RIDERS IN THE SKY

THE GHOSTS AND LEGENDS OF PHILMONT SCOUT RANCH

By Michael Connelly

Merril Press
Bellevue, Washington

Riders in the Sky

Riders in the Sky copyright © 2001 Michael R. Connelly. No part of this book may be reproduced in any form or by any electronic or mechanical means including information storage and retrieval systems without written permission, except in the case of brief quotations embodied in critical articles and reviews.

First Edition
Published by Merril Press
August 2001

Merril Press
Merril Mail Marketing, Inc.
P.O. Box 1682
Bellevue, Washington 98005
Telephone: 425-454-7009
Visit us at our website for additional copies ($12.00 each) of this title and others at www.merrilpress.com

Library of Congress Cataloging-in-Publication Data

Connelly, Michael, 1947-
   Riders in the sky : the ghosts and legends of Philmont Scout Ranch / Michael Connelly.--1st ed.
      p. cm.

   ISBN 0-936783-30-3
1. Ghosts -- New Mexico. 2. Philmont Scout Ranch. I. Title.

BF1472.U6 C66 2001
133.1'09789--dc21

                                        2001030876

PRINTED IN THE UNITED STATES OF AMERICA

For My Wife Kay

**My Love, My Inspiration, and My
Partner in Ghost Hunting**

Table of Contents

Introduction   i

1. Urraca Mesa   1

2. Baldy Town   25

3. Miranda   30

4. Ponil   40

5. Penitente Canyon   43

6. Rayado   48

7. French Henry Mine   57

8. Clarks Fork   59

9. Cyphers Mine   65

10. Dan Beard   70

11. The Spanish Lady   73

12. The Cimmaron Witch   75

13. The Santa Fe Trail   78

14. The Tooth of Time   81

15. The St. James Hotel   84

16. The Face in the Portrait   99

Epilogue   101

Acknowledgements   104

ILLUSTRATIONS

Cat Totem   x

The Shaman Who Guards the Mesa   12

The Skull of Urraca Mesa   24

Coffee with the Miner at Baldy Town   27

Teepees at Miranda   31

The Lady of the Meadow   35

A Little Girl's Lonely Grave   39

Kathleen's Piano   51

The Lonely Bugler Maintains His Vigil   53

The Gray Rider at Clarks Fork   61

The Restless Skull at Clarks Fork   64

The Tooth of Time   83

The St. James Hotel   85

T.J.'s Room   91

INTRODUCTION

To thousands of scouts and adult leaders it is a place known simply as "God's Country." Its official name is Philmont Scout Ranch and it is located in northeastern New Mexico, right outside of the small historic town of Cimarron. The ranch's over two hundred and forty-six square miles consist of hundreds of miles of trails which cross majestic mountains, ford crystal rivers, and wind through lush meadows. Wildlife is abundant and on their ten-day backpacking treks scouts may encounter elk, deer, or bears. At night they are often lulled to sleep by the song of the coyote. It is truly a scouting paradise, and it may also be the most haunted place in the world.

To consider the validity of that claim, it is first necessary to be familiar with the history of Philmont, a history that includes the world's largest dinosaurs, cowboys and Indians, gold miners and lumbermen, pioneer families, outlaws and lawmen. Archeological sites abound at Philmont, and the Boy Scouts of America has a staff of full time archeologists who supervise the digs and teach the scouts about the ranch's history.

It was these archeologists who confirmed an amazing discovery in 1995, the only known fossilized footprint of a Tyrannosaurus Rex in the world. These same scientists have also been actively engaged in studying the petroglyphs and other artifacts of the Anasazi Indians, "the ancient ones", who were the first known humans to inhabit the area thousands of years ago. The Anasazi in the Philmont area and other parts of New Mexico abruptly disappeared around nine hundred years ago for reasons never completely understood by archeologists. It is apparent, however, that their disappearance was preceded by a period of violent upheaval that led to the brutal deaths of many Anasazi by means of prolonged torture. Whether this was caused by an invasion of another tribe, such as the Toltec from Mexico, or some madness that caused the ancient ones to turn on each other, is unknown.

The Navajo were the next people in the area, and they were the first to discover traces of the culture of the ancient ones and the first to believe that the area was one where evil spirits dwelled and must be contained. They erected the legendary "cat totems" atop Urraca Mesa and left an aged medicine man to guard them, so the demons could not escape. The Navajo didn't stay long because they feared the mesa and they feared the warlike Jicarilla Apaches, who themselves feared little, except apparently the mesa, which remains taboo to their tribe and other Native American people in the vicinity.

The Spanish came next in the fifteen hundreds and set about subduing both the wild land and the native peoples, which proved to be no easy task. Bloody battles were fought in the Philmont area with neither side prepared to give quarter; but neither the Spaniards nor the Indians would ultimately be dominant because the Anglos soon began to arrive.

The first of these were the legendary mountain men, who roamed the Santa Cristo Mountains, living their solitary lives and trapping the numerous beaver in the Cimarron and Rayado Rivers. They disturbed little and generally shared the land peacefully with the Apaches and other area tribes. However, their dominion was also a brief one due to the fact that merchants soon blazed the famous Santa Fe Trail, a heavily traveled primitive highway which can still be seen today by scouts hiking in the Philmont back country. Settlers followed the merchants and to the rugged individualistic mountain men, these signs of encroaching civilization meant it was time to move on.

What is now New Mexico was still part of old Mexico during this period. In 1841, the Governor of Mexico deeded approximately 1.7 million acres of land to Charles Beaubien, a transplanted Canadian, and Guadalupe Miranda, a Mexican citizen. It was the largest land grant in American history. Ultimately Lucien Maxwell, who married one of the Beaubien daughters, acquired it and it is often referred to as the Maxwell Land Grant.

In 1846, war broke out between Mexico and the United States. U.S. forces quickly occupied the New Mexico territory. Many U.S. citizens were already living in the territory, but the transition was still not an easy one with the Anglo culture competing for dominance with the Spanish/Mexican culture. There also remained a large population of various Indian tribes who continued to resent the presence of both groups of interlopers.

One of the first attempts to establish a permanent settlement in the area was along the Rayado River in what is now part of Philmont. Charles Beaubien had tried setting up colonies before on his massive land grant, but none had been particularly successful. However, the ranch at Rayado was under the management of the capable Lucien Maxwell and he soon attracted others to join him, such as the famous frontiersman, Kit Carson, who built a large compound on the site of what is now the Kit Carson Museum.

The primary problem for settlements in the region was the raiding bands of Indians that continuously plagued them. Settlements were raided by roving war parties of Utes, Comanches, Apaches, and Kiowas. Some war parties had as many as six hundred warriors in them. The situation became so bad that a detachment of United States Dragoons was sent to Rayado in 1849. A permanent military post was established there about a year later.

Eventually, after considerable blood was shed on both sides, the Indians were subdued. A reservation was established for the Utes and Jicarilla Apaches near the frontier town of Cimarron. The reservation was a mistake from the beginning with two tribes which had long been enemies trying to live together while their traditional hunting grounds were being overrun by ranchers. However, the reservation stayed relatively peaceful from 1861 until 1867 when gold was discovered in the region. The rapid influx of fortune seekers caused not only the growth of Cimarron, but meant new towns were soon springing up, putting even more pressure on the Indian agency.

On the reservation, the Indians were treated in the same manner as on most reservations of the period. Promises were made, only to be immediately broken, and rations and blankets were often in short supply. To make matters worse, Anglos, sometimes even Indian agents themselves, persisted in selling whiskey to the Indians. It was a volatile situation that finally exploded in 1875 when a group of drunken Apaches refused to accept meat, which they claimed was contaminated. Gunfire erupted and the Indian agent, Alexander G. Irvine was wounded. The Apaches prepared for war, and the army moved in. When one of the Apaches was arrested, and later killed while trying to grab a weapon from a soldier, a prolonged violent conflict seemed inevitable.

The situation was peacefully resolved by the arrival of General Nelson A. Miles from Fort Union. He was very sympathetic to the plight of the Utes and Apaches and finally got the government to move the two tribes to different areas which were much more hospitable. His actions undoubtedly prevented a war that could have lasted for years.

While the Indian situation was being resolved other problems had developed in the broad area now known as Colfax County, New Mexico. Much of the original land grant was occupied by lumbermen, farmers and miners, many of whom had very little, if any, legal claim to the sites they were using. When Maxwell sold the bulk of his grant to the British dominated Maxwell Land Grant and Railway Company in 1870, a virtual war broke out between the two groups over how big the grant was and who owned what.

There were deaths on both sides, most notably that of the Reverend F. J. Tolby, a Methodist minister, allegedly killed because he sided with the anti-land grant group. His death led to others. The threat of continuous violence that could permanently destroy the chance for everyone in the county to gain prosperity became reality. Two new leaders emerged: the Reverend O. P. McMains, as leader of the settlers, and Frank Springer, as the representative of the now Dutch controlled land grant company.

Both men saw the necessity of stopping the violence and letting the courts resolve the matter. It was not until 1887 that the U.S. Supreme Court handed down a decision affirming that the company did, in fact, own the bulk of the land conveyed to it by Maxwell. The settlers had lost their case and slowly peace and prosperity returned to Colfax County.

Much of the land changed hands over the years as mines played out, logging operations ran their course, and ranches were sold or divided up. In 1937, Oklahoma oilman Waite Phillips gave 35,000 acres to the Boy Scouts of America for a camp to be named Philturn Rocky Mountain Scout Camp. He increased his donation to 127,000 acres in 1941 and the camp became known as Philmont Scout Ranch. Other acreage has been acquired since then, and the ranch is now the largest youth camp of its kind in the world. Over 20,000 scouts and leaders a year go on backpacking adventures at the ranch, which now has a seasonal staff of over 800.

Boy Scouts and both male and female Explorer Scouts fourteen years of age and older spend eleven days backpacking in the Philmont back country, carrying their own food and equipment and traveling through some of the most beautiful country in the world. Sometimes they just camp at designated sites along the trail while other nights are spent at staff camps where they can enjoy programs ranging from rock climbing to horseback riding and fly fishing.

It is undoubtedly because of the historical back drop described above that some of these scouts soon discover that they are not the only ones occupying Philmont. For whatever reason, many of the original inhabitants have chosen not to leave. They remain, and have become as much a part of Philmont as the horses and buffalo.

The stories in this book are not your ordinary ghost stories told around the campfire. Those are mostly stories of unknown origin that have passed from scout camp to scout camp over the years, often losing their original identity in the process. The ghosts at Philmont are not shy. They manifest themselves on a regular basis and have been seen, heard, and felt by hundreds of people over the years. When I went to Philmont to research this book, I talked with many people who had ghostly experiences that summer, which were virtually identical to the experiences reported to me on my backpacking trips to the ranch in 1991, 1996, and 1998.

It is up to you to decide if you want to believe the stories you are about to read. People who have experienced the events first hand or heard them directly from participants narrated many of the stories to me. Others have been handed down over the years, but with surprisingly little variation. Many of the names of participants are fictitious, either to protect their privacy or because the names have been lost and only the events remembered.

The facts themselves are apparently not fictitious, but frighteningly true, at least for those who were there and experienced them. I for one believe, because I have seen the look in the eyes and heard the fear in the voices of those who told me of their strange encounters with Philmont's formidable force of spirits.

If you remain skeptical after reading this book, I suggest you talk to my oldest son, Sean, who was probably the biggest skeptic I knew when it came to things that go bump in the night. That attitude changed quickly and permanently after two incidents occurred within the first several weeks of his employment as a wrangler at Philmont in the summer of 1995. He now agrees with many others and me. Philmont Scout Ranch is, in fact, the most haunted place in the world.

ONE

URRACA MESA

In July 1998, I was the advisor for a crew of five scouts and three adults hiking to Urraca Mesa from the south. It was my first trip to the mesa since my previous two crews had hiked in Philmont's north country. The mesa was a magnificent vista. It was also a formidable obstacle since we were coming from New Abreu Camp at an elevation of 7,248 feet and were going to have to climb to its height of over 8,500 feet.

As we crossed the last meadow before our arduous ascent, I was the third man in line. The crew chief, Steve Gilkey, was leading the file, with my nephew Ryan Connelly right behind him. Suddenly, out of nowhere, a three-foot long diamondback rattle snake slide between my nephew's legs and struck at me. Because those behind me claimed I jumped at least five feet in the air, a claim I do not dispute, his fangs missed my shin by a few inches. Then, just as quickly as he appeared, he was gone.

After a moment, we continued our trek toward the mesa, undaunted by what appeared to be one of the occasional dangers one will encounter at Philmont. However, my thoughts did drift to some of the 35
stories I had heard about the place we were approaching, and I could not help wondering if we had just received a warning. After all, the mesa does not particularly welcome visitors, as the reader will soon learn.

THE LOST SCOUT

Ben James had just finished his junior year at the United States Naval Academy in that summer of 1990. To his delight, he was assigned to spend the summer at Philmont working as a ranger, just as many cadets fom the military academies are. He had no complaints; he considered the job of ranger to be one of the best jobs at Philmont. He knew that the hard hiking would keep his muscular, six foot one inch frame in good physical shape for the rigors of his senior year at Annapolis.

In a nutshell, Ben's job as a ranger was to take incoming crews, consisting of seven to twelve scouts and adult leaders, and get them ready to spend eleven days backpacking in the mountains. He would spend a day with them at base camp preparing them for their trek. Then he would head out with them for one to three days in the back country making sure they became competent in such skills as map and compass reading, no impact camping, and first aid; all necessary if they were to have a safe and enjoyable Philmont experience. Once satisfied with their level of expertise, he would hike back to the base camp to pick up another incoming crew.

On one particularly hot and dry July afternoon, he left a crew to go on its way in the ranch's south country and was on his way back to the base camp. His route required him to cross Urraca Mesa, a rather difficult climb, but one that rarely daunted a ranger as conditioned as he was. As he reached the top of the mesa and started along the trail through the heavy growth of trees and brush, which would take him to the north side of the mesa where he would descend to Urraca Camp, he was not even thinking of the stories he had heard about the mesa. He discounted them anyway.

Upon entering a small clearing, Ben suddenly sensed a presence behind him. At the same moment, he was shoved violently from behind. He hit the ground rolling and came up ready to either protect himself from further attack or admonish some camper silly enough to play a joke on a ranger moving in full stride. However, there was no one for him to either fight or chew out. The clearing was empty.

As he looked around for any way his attacker could have escaped so quickly, he realized that no one was that fast, and finally taking a few deep breaths, he decided that his own imagination was running amok. He must simply have tripped over a rock. He adjusted his pack and turned to continue his journey. But after taking just a few steps, he was hit again from behind; this time more violently than before.

When he landed face first on the rocky ground, the air exploded from his lungs. For several minutes he lay there gasping for breath and feared a further assault, which he would be unable to repel. However, nothing more happened. He eventually rose shakily to his feet, and in a halting manner caused by his attempts to look every direction at once, exited the clearing and made it to the trail down the mesa without further mishap.

He mentioned the incident to no one at the base camp. But, he clearly felt that he was not welcome at the mesa and decided to try to avoid it whenever possible. Unfortunately, just two weeks later, he found himself in the position of having to cross the mesa again, this time at night. He had been assigned temporarily to a crew that had lost one of its two required adult advisors to a sprained ankle. After several days mending at base camp, the man was able to rejoin the crew. Ben was told that he needed to pick up a new crew immediately. The quickest way back was across the mesa.

The young ranger had endured much as a cadet at the Naval Academy, but nothing had prepared him for this. He knew there was something beyond his comprehension on Urraca, something malevolent, yet he was under orders to return quickly and that meant he had to summon up all of his courage and meet the challenge of crossing this ominous piece of terrain. After he had climbed the south wall and began to cross the mesa's flattop, he immediately noticed the complete silence. There were none of the usual night sounds associated with Philmont, no birds or insects chirping or buzzing, no howling coyotes, and not even the slightest breeze to stir the leaves on the thick stands of trees.

Ben moved as rapidly as he could without the aid of a flashlight, fearing that any illumination would attract attention to him. That was exactly what he did not need. Suddenly, he noticed a flicker of light on his right, thirty or forty yards off the trail. Freezing in place and watching carefully, he finally realized that he was seeing the dancing flames of a campfire, a campfire where none should be since there are no campsites on top of the mesa.

Leaving the trail and approaching cautiously, Ben saw a small campfire tended by a tow headed youngster of about fifteen. As he got closer Ben noticed two things; first that the boy was quietly sobbing, and second, that he was wearing a scout uniform from the mid 1940s, meaning that the uniform was almost fifty years old.

As he stepped within the circle of light generated by the fire, the ranger spoke quietly in order not to startle the boy.

"Are you okay?" he asked. "Can I help you?"

The boy failed to respond as Ben removed his pack and sat down on a log across from the youngster. However, the lad did look up and Ben knew he was looking into the most frightened pair of blue eyes he had ever seen. The boy's face was deathly pale in the firelight, the only highlights were smudges of dirt on his cheeks and what appeared to be a badly healing cut on his chin.

"Are you lost?" inquired Ben. "Did you get separated from your crew?"

The answer was obvious of course, but the young scout nodded slightly anyway, his first real acknowledgment that he was even aware of the ranger's existence.

"All right," said the ranger. "I'm on my way to base camp. Grab your gear and I'll lead you there."

Without waiting for an answer, Ben stood up and turned his back on the boy in order to pick up his pack. From behind him he heard the softly spoken words, "I can't."

Ben abruptly found himself in total darkness again. Spinning around he saw no fire and no small boy, only the darkness and dead silence of the mesa. Now he was both confused and frightened. He knew he was not dreaming, but when he took his flashlight out and searched the area, he found no trace that there had ever been a campfire in the area. Throwing caution to the wind, he used his light to get him off the mesa as soon as possible.

This time when he reached the ranger station at base camp he told his story and was informed that he had encountered the "Lost Scout", a young man who had disappeared on Urraca years before and never been found. He learned that there had been another sighting earlier in the summer, a duplicate of other incidents reported almost every summer.

One of those occurred when Ray Warren, a no nonsense forty-five year old scoutmaster from Oklahoma was leading his crew across the mesa early one morning. It was going to be a typical Philmont day. The sun had cut the morning chill and now it was warm and clear offering a spectacular view of the surrounding countryside from the top of the mesa. Ray's crew only admired the view for a few minutes however, because they were anxious to get to Urraca Camp at the northern base of the mesa.

As they rounded a bend in the trail, they were stopped in their tracks by a young scout who suddenly appeared on the trail in front of them. Ray immediately noticed the old uniform that the boy was wearing and knew without asking that the boy was lost and frightened. As was the case with Ben, the lad spoke little, simply saying that he was lost.

Ray offered the young scout both food and water that he declined with a shake of his head. The members of Ray's crew just stood staring at this strange boy because, like Ray, they felt there was something that did not seem right. The whole thing was surreal, as if the entire crew was sharing the same weird dream. They were not about to leave a fellow scout however, and Ray instructed him to fall in with the crew.

The crew resumed its trek and the boy kept up the pace, walking silently, his head down, looking more like a whipped dog than anything else. When they reached the edge of the mesa the crew took a break before beginning their descent and their guest again silently refused any water from the offered canteens. Ray just shook his head in confusion. He believed the boy was in some kind of shock and was looking forward to getting him down to the camp where he could be transported to base camp and get help from professionals.

After a ten minute break the crew donned their packs and started down the trail off the mesa. The crew leader was in the lead and Ray was right behind him. They had only gone a few steps when the advisor heard a startled yell from behind him and then several of the boys began calling his name. Ray stopped the crew and started back up the trail only to find some very shaken members of his group.

"Mr. Warren," blurted one of the boys. "The kid's gone! He was walking right in front of me and he just disappeared."

"I saw it too." said another boy. "He didn't fall or leave the trail; he was just gone. He disappeared just as he reached the edge of the mesa."

While trying to calm his shaken crewmembers, Ray glanced around. There was no place for the boy to have gone or hidden in the immediate area.

Ray led a search but when nothing was found, he took his crew to Urraca Camp where he reported the incident. When he described the boy, the staff informed him of the nature of this phantom scout, and although another search was launched, everyone knew he would not be found.

Ray kept one thing to himself that day however, because he wasn't sure if it had been real, or just his over-active imagination. As he had started his crew down the trail after their fruitless search he had glanced back up the trail and thought he saw the young scout standing at the edge of the mesa, tears streaming down his face and his hand raised in a plaintive farewell wave. The reason he did not stop and go back was because he could not trust what his own senses were telling him he was seeing. The boy, who had seemed so real before was now virtually transparent, more a wisp of smoke than a person and as Ray looked on the scout faded away altogether.

The "Lost Scout" continues to make his appearance on Urraca, reportedly trying several times each summer to attach himself to a crew crossing the mesa. Unfortunately, his spirit seems unable to leave the strange world he inhabits high up on the spot where demons are said to dwell.

THE SHAMAN

Urraca Camp is a beautiful campsite located in the woods on the edge of a broad meadow. It is a staff camp providing a challenge course for the crews that stop there as well as the Philmont story campfire program at night. It is reported to be located at the base of the mesa rather than on top because no local contractors could be found who would work on top of its foreboding heights. However, being at the base of the mesa has not kept the camp from being subjected to its influences.

During June of 1997, the camp director at Urraca Camp was Ron Walker, a short heavy set junior in college who was working his third year at Philmont. He was just settling down in his cabin late one night when there were four loud knocks on his front door. Climbing wearily from his bunk, he opened the door expecting to find another staff member or a camper with some kind of problem; instead, there was no one there. He was sure that someone was playing a prank, and he had had a long day and was not in the mood, so he closed the heavy wooden door and waited for the inevitable repeat performance. It came just seconds later, four loud knocks. He jerked open the door immediately, expecting to catch someone, but again the porch was empty.

Now he was truly puzzled because the porch runs the full length of the front of the cabin with steps at either end and heavy wooden rails along its front. There was no way that anyone was fast enough to get off that porch without him seeing them or at least hearing their footsteps. Yet, the porch and the meadow in front of it, which were well illuminated by the full moon, were indeed empty. As Ron stepped back into the cabin and closed the door there were suddenly four loud knocks on the rear wall of the cabin. Before Ron could even approach the back window, he heard the same series of raps on one side of the cabin and then again on the front door.

In fact, the rapping was now circling the cabin, four knocks each occurring on the walls and the front door. They repeated more rapidly now, faster than any human could run around the cabin. Eventually there was just a continuous noise, almost a roar, and the walls seemed ready to buckle under the onslaught.

Even a seasoned Philmont veteran like Ron was having trouble dealing with this, and holding his ears and stifling a scream, the camp director backed into his bedroom and crouched down on the floor trying to will this thing, whatever it was, back up on top of the mesa where it belonged. Yet, the violent assault on the cabin continued until Ron yelled out the only two words, which came into his mind, "Thank you!" Then there was silence.

It took him a few minutes to adjust to this new phenomenon, and then he realized why the phrase he had yelled had had such an immediate effect. The knocking was the signal of the old Navajo shaman, assigned centuries ago to protect the cat totems on the mesa. The rapping was the number four repeated over and over again, a noisy, but effective notification by the shaman's spirit that he is still on the job. The camp director knew now that the stories he had heard were true and he laid awake the rest of the night reliving the legend in his head.

Ron was well aware that the Anasazi Indians were the first to occupy the mesa, hundreds, perhaps even thousands of years before. Yet, while some of their artifacts and petroglyphs have been found, no one has ever been able to explain the apparent sudden disappearance of the tribe from Philmont and other locations in northern New Mexico. No mass grave sites have been found, and no indications of plague, yet something or someone drove them away in a very short period of time. How could an entire people suddenly vanish?

There are numerous theories propounded by archeologists and anthropologists, about which they argue endlessly, but no clear answer has emerged. However, the Navajo may have discovered at least part of the answer several hundred years ago. They left no record of what they found, but something caused them to determine that Urraca Mesa is the gateway to the underworld, where only demons dwell. They ceremonially sealed the mesa to contain these demons by erecting four cat totems, one on each corner of the mesa. These intricately carved totems contain symbols understood only by the Navajo and their presence is simply to keep the demons from escaping. As long as one still stands, the people of the earth will be protected from the wrath of the underworld.

However, the Navajo apparently took a further precaution; to protect the cat totems, they left their most powerful shaman to guard them and he is still there today. He has been seen by hundreds of people, appearing often in the form of a blue ball of light. Those individuals brave enough to approach the light will see him standing in the middle of it in full regalia, wearing a decorated buckskin shirt and leggings and a head dress of buffalo horns. His hair is gray and braided and his face is worn and creased with age, the eyes are alert and watchful. On some occasions, he will appear as one of his alter egos, such as a bear, panther, or wolf. He has never been known to harm anyone, but with only two of the totems still remaining he appears to be getting more aggressive in trying to scare people away from their locations. Even during the day, photographs taken of the mesa will often show a strange blue light.

Several weeks after Ron had his strange experience and his sleepless night he learned that he was not the first staff member to be in the cabin when the Shaman came knocking and he would not be the last. He also learned about others who have had experiences on top of the mesa.

RIDERS IN THE SKY

The Anasazi knew nothing of horses since their disappearance predated the introduction of the animals by the Spanish. Subsequent Native American tribes in the area did have the animals, but since the mesa has long been taboo to the tribes, there is no reason to believe that any of them kept horses on the mesa. There is also no record of any ranchers losing a herd of horses in the area, yet there is a ghost herd which not only roams the mesa but other parts of Philmont as well.

No one has ever seen the herd, but its presence has been made known in other ways. Whether it is a herd of wild mustangs, or the ghostly remnants of a lost band of Indian warriors or a missing cavalry patrol is the subject of speculation. Perhaps they are the legendary "Riders in the Sky" made famous in western lore by both song and campfire tale. Whatever their origin, they are a ghostly force to be avoided according to those Philmont staffers who have encountered them.

One of the most recent and dramatic incidents occurred in 1995 and involved two wranglers, Sean Connelly and his friend Tim. It was Sean's first year working at Philmont. But he had been on a trek there in 1991 and had heard the stories about Urraca Mesa. He was determined to find out for himself if there was any truth to them. He knew about the Shaman and the lost scout and he had also been told about the herd of horses. Therefore he and Tim decided to camp on the mesa on their day off.

Neither of these young men was easily spooked. Sean was a junior in college, a qualified army paratrooper, and a professional rodeo cowboy who rode both bulls and saddle broncos on weekends. He was slightly shorter than Tim was, but ruggedly handsome and in fine physical shape. Tim was tall, slender and equally athletic with a background in ranch work and a love of the outdoors, which matched that of Sean.

The two wranglers left the base camp in the early afternoon and made it to the top of the mesa in time to experience one of the glorious sunsets for which Philmont is famous. The night was going to be beautiful and clear and the two cowboys decided to meadow crash, Philmont vernacular for sleeping under the stars. Just after they had set their packs down and begun to get ready to eat their dinner, Sean heard what sounded like the thunder of scores of hooves in the distance. He asked his friend if he could hear anything and Tim replied he heard nothing.

Believing his imagination was getting the best of him, Sean proceeded with his meal preparations and tried to ignore the sounds that continued to grow louder and more distinct. He was clearly hearing a large horse herd and he again questioned Tim and received a negative reply.

The noises continued, growing louder and louder and Sean knew that within minutes the stampeding herd would be on top of them.

"Tim, can't you hear the horses?" asked Sean.

"No," replied Tim nervously, "but let's get out of here!"

The boys scrambled to stow their gear and headed for the trail down the mesa when they were frozen in their tracks. Standing ahead of them next to the trail was the outline of a man, clearly an Indian, since even in the darkness they could make out the full horned headdress. Both wranglers automatically switched on their flashlights only to see nothing in the strong beams.

They had no time to search for this strange apparition however, because the phantom herd was still thundering down on them and they started out quickly for the rim of the mesa. It took only seconds for them to realize that the mysterious figure of the Indian was still with them, his silhouette just off the trail, matching their long strides.

When they finally reached the rim and started down, the sounds of the horses suddenly stopped and were replaced by a silence broken only by the noise of their boots striking the ground and their own labored breathing. The Indian was still with them, paralleling their march, his moving figure clearly seen except when they shined a light his way, which revealed only endless darkness. After a hike they feared would never end, they reached the base of the mesa and looked for their Native American companion. He was no longer with them. The Shaman had escorted them off the mesa, out of harm's way, but also away from his precious totems. For that night, at least, the ghost of the old Indian could rest; he had done his job, and done it well, at least as far as the two wranglers were concerned.

BOSS

He was known simply as Boss since he had been in charge of the wranglers at Philmont for a number of years. He worked the ranch full time with a few other year round wranglers and they maintained the herds of cattle, horses, and buffalo through the long and often severely cold winter months when the part time summer staff were gone.

Boss was a likable fellow, outgoing and easy to get along with. At that time, some of the ranch's cattle and horses were kept on the mesa during the summer because of the excellent grazing. On a crisp fall day about twenty years ago, Boss saw what appeared to be an early winter storm developing on the other side of Urraca Mesa. Since it was several weeks before the scheduled move of the herds to their winter pasture, he informed the other cowboys that he was going to ride up on the mesa and check the herds.

He left late in the morning for what should have been a quick trip, but he failed to return in the afternoon. Even after it grew dark, the other wranglers were not alarmed since Boss was known to ride into town sometimes at the end of the day for a few beers at one of the Cimarron saloons. However, a trip into town later that night by some of his companions failed to turn him up.

Now there was a growing concern among the other cowboys and a search of the mesa was launched the next morning. No trace of Boss or his mount were located on top of Urraca so the search was widened to the area around the mesa; but after three days the searchers had still found nothing. Both the rescuers and their mounts were exhausted but Boss's friends were not ready to give up yet. Two of them had returned to their headquarters for remounts so they could continue the search. They had grabbed a quick cup of coffee and a hand full of beef jerky and were saddling up their new horses in the corral when they noticed a lone rider coming across the meadow. The man wore no hat and was sporting a mop of unruly white hair. He looked so thin that he appeared almost emaciated. The wranglers knew of no one fitting this description, yet something about the approaching figure made them very uneasy.

It was not until he was almost on top of them that they realized to their horror that it was Boss, reduced from a healthy and robust figure with dark brown hair to this scarecrow of a man in just three days. He could barely stand as they helped him from his horse and into the bunkhouse. They repeatedly asked him what had happened and where he had been but he remained silent. Much to everyone's relief Boss recovered his health in several weeks, but he continued to refuse to discuss what happened to him on the mesa and he never went near it again.

He is reportedly still alive and retired in the Cimarron area. His hair remains an albino white and he still will tell no one of his experiences on Urraca. However, old timers speculate that if in fact there is a gateway to hell on the mesa, Boss may have wondered into it by accident and been confronted by sights too terrible to remember, much less talk about.

THE MISSING RANGER

Jim Taylor was not your typical Philmont ranger. He was short and heavy set with a pasty complexion, which never seemed to darken no matter how much time he spent in the sun. He looked like he belonged on a job in his home town computer store rather than working outdoors in the often harsh environment of Philmont, but he had passed all of the tests and seemed to be doing all right in that summer of 1983. It was his second year as a ranger, but it was not long into the summer that problems began.

He was constantly asking questions about Urraca Mesa, to the point of being an annoyance to those fellow staff members who had told him the same stories over and over again. On the mesa itself, his behavior was reported by both fellow rangers and crewmembers to be increasingly erratic. He would often talk to himself and his eyes never stopped moving, as if looking for something which no one else could see.

He became sloppy with his dress and his personal hygiene. Instead of teaching his crews about the basics of wilderness camping, he spent much of his time talking about the demons on Urraca and how they would soon be loose. Then one day he snapped completely while escorting a crew across the mesa, using vile language and yelling threats at the terrified crewmembers as he ran in a circle around them. Abruptly he stopped, his huge staring eyes looking at something behind the crew. As they turned and saw nothing, Jim let go with a horrible scream and his face contorted into a mask of pure terror. He threw off his pack and took off running, all the while screaming back over his shoulder that they were coming for him.

When the crew made it to the next staff camp, Jim's breakdown and disappearance were reported and an immediate search was launched by Philsar (Philmont Search and Rescue), one of the most highly trained and skilled rescue operations in the world. As good as Philsar is, it is much more difficult to track down someone who does not want to be found, as was the case with Jim Taylor. As a result, the search was called off after a week. It was suddenly resumed several weeks later when a pair of rangers reported seeing Jim on Mt. Phillips. Once again, the elusive fugitive could not be located.

There were several more sightings over the remainder of the summer with the disturbed ranger reported to be even more ragged and downright terrifying in his appearance. Then, on a rainy July day in 1984, Jim's body was found by a member of a passing crew. It was just off the trail, not far from where his journey had started. He was at the very base of the mesa.

His body had decomposed rapidly in the summer heat, but two things were apparent; the hair on his head was completely burned off and his boots had been melted to the flesh on his feet. It appeared he had been struck by lightening. Either that or he had been tortured by someone or something. Whatever the case, there have been numerous reports of a frightening figure of a young man, partially clothed in rags, and obviously burned, darting from tree to tree near the base of Urraca Mesa, as if attempting to still hide from the demons that chase him even beyond the grave.

THE NUMBERS GAME

Often when dealing with restless spirits, something will be found which appears to be of special significance to them like a particular room in a house or a particular object in a room. In the case of Urraca Mesa it appears that two numbers have special meaning, four and two twenty-two. The significance of the number four is obvious. The Navajo erected four cat totems to contain the demons. It was reported by the director at Urraca Camp that a series of four rapid knocks on his cabin signified the presence of the Shaman.

Matthew Vogel of East Lansing, Michigan was a staff member at Philmont in 1998 and before that, he had been with a crew, a crew that had crossed the mesa. Matt had heard the stories of the mesa and firmly believed that they were typical of the campfire stories that he had heard for years as a Boy Scout, in other words, he believed none of them.

When his crew camped at Urraca Mesa they attended the campfire program prepared by the staff, and Matt for the first time heard about the mysterious knocks on the staff cabin always consisting of four raps in increasingly rapid succession. He easily dismissed that story too, at least until the next morning when his crew climbed to the top of the mesa and set off across it.

It was a beautiful morning, clear and cool in the high altitude. Matt heard a crow cawing above them and looked up to see the largest crow he had ever seen, circling his crew. A chill gripped Matt's body because he suddenly knew, for no apparent reason, that this enormous bird was no ordinary crow.

Matt listened closer to its cry and realized that the crow was cawing four times, then pausing and cawing four times again. Matt counted the seconds between the sequences of four and found exactly a four second interval between each one. The crow continued to circle the scouts and cry its warning until the crew had safely left the mesa.

The story behind the number two twenty-two is more obscure. One legend among some of the Indian tribes, which still inhabit the area around Philmont, is that a fierce battle was fought between the Lord of the Underworld and his brother, the Lord of the Overworld for the spirits of the Anasazi. The Lord of the Overworld won and banished his brother and his demons back to the underworld. The battle is believed to have concluded at 2:22 in the morning.

There is, of course, no way of confirming this legend, however, numerous campers and staff members report that when camping around the mesa, they wake up at 2:22 a.m. for no reason which anyone can determine. Luke Teske reports this happening to him when he was camping at the mesa with a ranger training crew.

This author has personally been on three treks at Philmont and the one thing which was an absolute certainty was that I would be so exhausted at the end of the day that I would sleep through the night, never stirring until the crew chief woke me up the next morning. At least that was always the case until my third trek in 1998, when we camped at Urraca Camp. I woke up at exactly 2:22, and never knew what had disturbed me. However, I was concerned enough to check the camp, and as I walked around, I heard both boys and advisors stirring in every tent. It was clear that everyone had awakened at 2:22 a.m.

THE SKULL

Those who have ghostly experiences on or around the mesa need no confirmation that it is indeed haunted. However, even the skeptics are often astonished and a little shaken when they look at the mesa on a topographic map of Philmont. The highest part of Urraca Mesa is seen as an almost perfect profile of a human skull. Many say that if you look very closely, you can also see what appears to be an additional shape of a small human figure in the eye of the skull.

Some believe it is the Navajo Shaman maintaining his lonely vigil over the mesa. Others believe it is the Lord of the Underworld, standing ready to let loose his minions when the last cat totem falls. If that is in fact the case, I for one do not believe I would care to be hiking across Urraca mesa when that event occurs.

TWO

BALDY TOWN

BALDY TOWN HOTEL

Baldy Camp is located at the former site of Baldy Town. It is one of the jumping off points for crews wishing to climb Baldy Mountain, the highest peak on Philmont at 12,441 feet. Baldy Town was a prosperous mining community that was occupied off and on from 1868 until 1940. Many of its residents worked the Aztec mine, one of the most famous gold mines in the United States.

Baldy Camp is now the site of a trading post and commissary and the home to a rather rambunctious group of former residents. Mining towns were notorious for their nightlife, with the miners spending their wages on various nefarious activities, few of which were illegal in communities with no law. And, of course, there were always those enterprising types ready and eager to separate the miners from their cash.

One such location in Baldy Town was the Baldy Town hotel with its famous saloon where miners and travelers to the town could drink, gamble, and find female companionship. The hotel's rooms could be rented by the hour, the day, or the week, but it was unusual to get much sleep since the saloon would not settle down until dawn. However, it was the best, and only, hotel in town.

Unfortunately for Kathy Gilmore, a petite brunette from Cleveland, Ohio, her staff tent was pitched right on the old foundation of the Baldy Town Hotel when she came to work at Philmont in the summer of 1994. Kathy had been on staff for several years, but this was her first assignment to Baldy Camp and she was looking forward to it. She was working in the trading post. The first day had been a bit crazy; with all of the shelves needing to be stocked and preparations made for the influx of campers the next week. She was exhausted when she settled down in her tent for the night, but expected to be undisturbed until morning, since as the only female staff member at Baldy Camp, she had a tent to herself. She certainly did not expect to be awakened by the sounds of shouts and gunfire, but that was exactly what happened at 3:15 in the morning.

She thought she had been dreaming at first, but as she lay in her bunk, three more gunshots followed the first two that had awakened her. There were also several more screams and then silence. Kathy could not believe someone was shooting at Baldy Camp, especially this time of the morning. She did not know whether to leave her tent and investigate or just wait until someone came to tell her what was going on. She chose the latter course of action, or in this case, inaction, but all she heard from the camp was continued silence.

When she reached the point that she could stand it no more she ventured from her tent to find the camp just as it had been when she retired. It was breezy and cold and there wasn't a cloud in the sky; nor was there any carnage in the street or any other evidence of disturbance. She decided she must have dreamed it after all and decided just to keep the whole thing to herself.

The next day was as busy as the first with the staff working late into the night, and Kathy was even more exhausted when she finally made it to her tent. However, this time she had not even had a chance to close her eyes before she heard the sounds of boisterous laughter, piano music, and terrible off key singing. She thought the rest of the staff must still be up partying without her and slipping back into her clothes and prepared to go to the staff cabin and ask them to quiet down. To her amazement, when she left the tent the sounds stopped and she realized they had not been coming from the staff cabin, but from right outside of her tent. She decided then that her rest was being disturbed by the noises of history; cowboys, miners and ladies of the evening, who despite the fact that the Baldy Town Hotel and saloon were long gone, continued to engage in their nightly revelry and occasional violence.

The next day the young Ohio State University student had her tent moved to another location. To her surprise, there were no wise cracks from her fellow staff members when she explained the reasons for her move. They had all worked at Baldy Camp before and had all, on more than one occasion been passing by the foundation of the old hotel and heard the ghostly voices of a bygone era.

THE COFFEE DRINKING MINER

One of the most amenable ghosts at Philmont is usually seen in the early morning when the Baldy Town staff is helping themselves to their first cup of good strong frontier coffee. Sometimes this bearded, middle aged miner, wearing the clothing of the late 1800's will already be in the coffee room when they arrive, and other times will just appear.

He never has anything to say, but leans against the wall or the filing cabinet drinking his own mug of coffee and watching the goings on around him with a look of detached amusement. He appears in no hurry and will linger over his coffee for some time. When he is finished with his cup he just disappears, evidently heading for work in one of the long closed mines, or perhaps to just roam the area looking for his own mother lode.

Three

MIRANDA

The staff camp at Miranda is named after Guadalupe Miranda, one of the two men who received the original land grant of the area in 1841 from the governor of Mexico. The area was heavily mined during the high points of the region's gold rush and was the site of a large placer mining operation. Placer mining involves the washing of sand and gravel to separate the gold and often entails the use of 'hydraulicking" - a method utilizing the spraying of a mountainside or ridge with water from high-pressure hoses to loosen the sand and gravel. This was a dangerous and environmentally destructive technique that led to one of the great tragedies of the area and left two of the most active and frequently seen spirits at Philmont.

THE HEADLESS CHILD

Since 1969 Miranda has been a pick up and drop off point for crews that want to experience a few days of burro packing. Burros are notoriously cantankerous and skittish so Jim Johnson, a lanky six foot two cowboy from Montana, who was a staff member in 1989, was not unduly surprised when a group of burros he was leading across the meadow to the Miranda corral began acting up. In fact, not only did all three of them refuse to move, they began backing up, tugging fiercely against their halters.

As Jim struggled with the animals and used some colorful language to question their parentage, he glanced around to see what might have stirred them up. That was when he noticed what appeared to be a young girl crossing the meadow. As the girl approached, the burros went berserk and Jim lost control. The animals broke loose and headed across the field away from the girl. When he looked back at her again, Jim suddenly knew why the animals had bolted. The child walking toward him wore a frilly white homespun dress that hung to her feet but left her arms bare. She was unwrinkled and unsoiled, perfect in every way, except that she had no head.

Jim was unable to move as the girl passed within a few feet of him, and he was unable to take his eyes off the raggedly torn flesh jutting from the neck of her dress where her head should have been. She continued across the trail and walked to the far edge of the meadow where she seemed to just sink into the ground.

The burros forgotten, the frightened wrangler headed for the staff cabin where he stammered out his tale to several other members of the Miranda staff. After calming him down as much as possible, the young man and young woman accompanied him back to the site where he had seen the girl disappear and they were shocked to find an old grave hidden in the tall grass right inside of the tree line. No grass grew on the grave and the soil had sunk in a few inches, but the grave was clearly outlined by a rectangle of gray stones. There was a badly worn wooden marker at its head. The marker was so badly worn by years of wind and rain that the name and dates were no longer visible, and it leaned drunkenly to one side.

After straightening the marker, the trio returned to the cabin where Jim immediately went to the radio and called in the code 10-1000 to the base camp. This is a Philmont emergency code that means, "Send a chaplain immediately". When the chaplain arrived he was taken to the grave site where after saying a short prayer for the little girl's restless spirit he was informed by Jim that he wanted to ride with the chaplain back to base camp, and from there head home. He had seen enough.

Research into the history of the surrounding area by various staff members has revealed that the ghost of the little girl is probably the daughter of one of the miners who worked at Miranda in the early 1900s. She was approximately ten years old when she wandered too close to the mining area one day. She was not noticed by the miners who turned on one of the high-pressure hoses to tear out sections of the ridge north of the camp. The child was instantly decapitated and her head was never found. Perhaps that is what she seeks.

Unfortunately, the chaplain's prayer seems to have had very little effect on the little girl's headless ghost. Since Jim's encounter, she has been seen several times wandering the meadow near the gravesite, but at least she is not alone in her quest, whatever it may be.

THE LADY OF THE MEADOW

The discovery of the grave and the subsequent research which revealed the probable identity of the pitiful little ghost, if not her name, also provided a possible explanation for another phenomenon which has been occurring at

Miranda for years; the appearance of the "Lady of the Meadow". The lady has been seen often, always dressed in white, and sometimes wearing a veil. She is believed to be the mother of the child who was killed because she is most frequently seen at or near the gravesite.

She is very protective of the grave and for some unknown reason seems to get particularly upset if the grave marker is righted, an experience repeatedly reported by staff members since the first misguided effort was made the day the grave was found. On the following day when one of the staff visited the grave, the marker was crooked again and was promptly righted for the second time. That evening when the staff returned to the cabin, they were stunned to find it in complete disarray. Food and cooking utensils were scattered all over the floor, obviously tossed about by someone in a great state of agitation.

On another occasion, a passing crew straightened the marker during the day. That night several staff members were sleeping in their teepees when they were awakened by a bright red light circling their canvas quarters. At first, believing it to be a camper with a flashlight, they emerged from the teepee only to see what appeared to be a brightly illuminated red ball circling faster and faster around the tent until it finally reached the top, where it hovered for a moment before speeding off in the direction of the meadow and the grave site. They followed as quickly as they could and then watched the fiery ball as it stopped over the gravesite for several minutes before disappearing. They had no problem

lem interpreting this strange event as a warning to leave the grave and its crooked marker alone.

The Lady of the Meadow is a very busy spirit, manifesting herself in numerous ways to both staff and campers. Mark Cradle reported that in 1998 he was assigned to one of the ten-day rotations as a wrangler at Miranda. The first thing the handsome Texas cowboy did upon arriving at his quarters next to the burro pen was to nail a horseshoe to a two by four so he could hang up his ropes. On the second night, he was awakened by the sound of the ropes flying off the horseshoe and hitting the ground. There was no one else present in the small room, and the ropes could not have fallen by themselves.

The next night Mark was lying in his bunk reading by the light of his oil lamp when it began to grow dim. He knew he had just filled the lamp with oil so he turned up the wick, only to have it go dim again. After this happened several more times he finally gave up and went to sleep. The following night when he began to experience the same problems he decided it must be the Lady of the Meadow so he apologized to her for intruding into her territory, but told her, "I'm only doing my job." She apparently understood and accepted this explanation because there were no more incidents during the rest of his rotation.

The veiled lady is not without a sense of humor however, and she can be a bit of a prankster. On one occasion, a wrangler was putting up some burros with the help of a camper. When the burros were all inside of the corral and the gate was securely closed, the wrangler stepped inside of the shack to hang up his ropes. When he came back outside, he was shocked to see the gate wide open and the burros wandering around freely outside of the corral. He angrily asked the young camper why he had opened the gate, and the boy calmly replied that he hadn't done it, the lady in the white dress had. When asked, "What lady?" the camper replied, "The one standing under the tree over there." The cowboy looked in the direction the camper was pointing and could see no one, but the youngster had described the Lady of the Meadow perfectly.

The lady can also attempt to be helpful at times. Two wranglers passing through Miranda on a glorious Friday afternoon decided to rest their mounts for a while so they hobbled their horses, loosened their cinches, and removed their bridles, hanging them in a nearby tree. They then headed for the cabin for a much needed cup of coffee. They saw no one approach the horses the whole time they sat drinking coffee on the porch of the staff cabin, yet when they returned to their horses, their cinches were tightened and the bridles were back on and they were ready to ride.

Miranda's most active guest is also ready and able to turn the tables on anyone who takes her presence too lightly. One summer two staff members decided to play a prank on a third staff member who, never having seen the lady himself, refused to believe in her existence. They went to town, found a brown wig and white dress and waited patiently that night until their friend headed for one of Philmont's heralded outdoor plumbing facilities. Once he entered the latrine, the shorter of the two pranksters donned the dress and wig and climbed up a tree that stood not far from the outhouse door. There he sat in plain sight on a limb while his companion hid behind the trunk.

When the object of the exercise emerged from the latrine, he was immediately greeted by the young man in white, sitting on a tree limb and wailing in a rather poor attempt to imitate a banshee. The young man appeared just startled at first and then clearly frightened, and he became increasingly agitated as he pointed up toward the tree. In fact, the youth seemed so badly shaken that the fraudulent lady pulled off the wig to let him know it was all just a joke.

Instead of calming the young staff member down however, this revelation only appeared to shake him up more, and he continued to point into the tree yelling, "Look, Look!" At that point, the perpetrators did look and saw the real Lady of the Meadow, sitting on a tree limb above them, and appearing to be enjoying herself immensely. The prank ended at that point with all three participants setting world record time in returning to the cabin.

FLOWERS ON THE GRAVE

Although the tragic figure of the little headless girl is not seen nearly as often as that of her mother, those who have heard her story frequently visit her grave. However, there is a warning attached to any such proposed excursion. According to Kyle Gadly, an ambulance driver at Philmont, it is a widely held belief that if you visit the grave, you must leave flowers at the site. Those who fail to do so always experience a wave of bad luck immediately thereafter.

It is also frequently reported that sometimes the staff will find fresh flowers on the grave, when no one has been around to place them there. These particular bundles of flowers will stay fresh and beautiful for as long as two weeks, a true phenomenon in light of the hot summer weather at Philmont.

FOUR

PONIL

What is now the staff camp at Ponil has a long history dating back to the time when it was a small community on the Cimarron and Northwest Railroad. It later became the ranch headquarters for Waite Phillips, and then the base camp for the original Philturn Scout Camp. It was also wrangler headquarters for a number of years, and as such, the home for many of Philmont's year-round staff and their families.

Scout crews that stop at Ponil during their treks are treated to horseback rides and taught to brand and rope. There is also a commissary, trading post and root beer cantina on site. Fishing is available along picturesque Ponil Creek and the campers are provided with a chuck wagon dinner and a pancake breakfast, a most pleasant change from the usual freeze-dried trail fare.

Ponil Camp is nestled in a beautiful little valley where five canyons converge and is a favorite campsite for crews hiking the North Country. It is also the home of one of Philmont's most famous ghost.

THE COWBOY IN THE BUNKHOUSE

Years ago when Ponil was still wrangler headquarters a cowboy who had lived and worked at Philmont almost from its beginning died in the Ponil bunkhouse. He had been gravely ill for several months with cancer. Since death was inevi-

death was inevitable, he chose to die at Ponil rather than among strangers in some far away hospital. On the day of his death, his friends and fellow wranglers, his only family, surrounded him. The telephone in the bunkhouse began ringing just as the cowboy breathed his last, but was ignored by his friends who comforted him until the end.

Every summer since his death, the wranglers report hearing the frequent ringing of a telephone in the bunkhouse. However, no one can ever answer the phone because it was removed from Ponil approximately ten years ago, and the nearest telephone is over twelve miles away.

One night in 1995, Sean Connelly was assigned to Ponil and had just climbed into his bed in the bunkhouse. His bunk was the one nearest to the door and he was surprised when the door opened since everyone else occupying the building was already asleep. There were no inside lights on, however, the open doorway let in the light of the full moon. As the door closed, Sean realized that there had been no one in the doorway. That is why he tensed up quickly when he heard the unmistakable sounds of someone wearing boots walking down the center of the big room.

The footsteps were heavy and clear. They continued to the end of the room where there was a momentary pause and then the steps reversed themselves and started back toward the door. The unseen figure passed Sean's bunk without stopping, and then the door opened and closed again as the intruder left. Again, Sean could see no one.

The next day the Louisiana cowboy learned that this is a frequent event in the bunkhouse. In addition, wranglers are often awakened by the sound of marbles rolling around on the table in the bunkhouse; however, they will find no marbles and no prankster. There has also been some activity under the bunkhouse itself. Some staff members refuse to work alone in the crawl space under the building, but will not talk about the reason.

FIVE

PENITENTE CANYON

About a mile and a half south of Ponil is Penitente Canyon. There are no established trails through the canyon and no campsites near it. It is forbidden territory to those who work at Philmont because, unlike Urraca Mesa, which is regularly visited despite its haunted reputation, the spirits who inhabit Penitente Canyon are so clearly malevolent that no one who has entered the canyon has failed to be physically and emotionally shaken by what they saw or felt.

The Philmont wranglers know for sure that they cannot enter the canyon, at least not on horseback. No Philmont horses or burros will set a hoof in the place, shying away violently if ridden anywhere near an entrance. Those cowboys who are brave enough to dismount and walk a few yards into the canyon don't stay for long; they report that the canyon is at least thirty degrees cooler than the areas outside, and the presence of evil can be felt hanging in the air like a thick fog.

THE LOST HIKER

The canyon is approximately a mile long and on the Philmont map appears to be a relatively easy hike of less than thirty minutes. At least that is what conservationist Bob Morgan thought when he topped a ridge and saw the canyon stretched out in front of him. He had a map, but no compass. He had lost the trail from

New Dean Camp to Ponil, and figured if he continued hiking in the general direction of the
morning sun he would eventually hit Ponil
Creek, which he could follow into the staff camp.
He did not know which canyon it was, but it
looked like an easy short cut because he
thought he could make out the other end from
where he was standing. It appeared to head in a
northeasterly direction and with its steep sides,
would keep him on a course consistent with
finding the creek.

As he entered the canyon, the blond, deeply
tanned outdoorsman immediately felt the chill in
the air and something else that had nothing to
do with the drop in temperature. He felt the hair
on the back of his neck stand up and a sudden
feeling of fear overtook him, as if he were being
warned away from this place. He almost turned
around at that point, but he was lost and knew
of no other way to find his way to Ponil, so he
took a few deep breaths and set out.

The further he ventured into the canyon the
more he began to have the strange feeling that
he was somewhere other than Philmont. The
canyon contained none of the natural beauty of
the rest of the ranch, the trees looked sick and
stunted and even the soil he walked on looked
black and somehow foreign. After hiking for half
an hour, he saw what appeared to be the other
end of the canyon a quarter of a mile ahead.
However, when another thirty minutes had
passed he began to notice that the end of the
canyon appeared no closer, but actually a little
farther away.

Since Bob had no other choices available to him he kept going and two hours later he panicked when he came on a set of human footprints in the dark soil and realized he had crossed his own trail. He was going in circles. "How could this be possible?" he asked himself aloud, as if the sound of his own voice could dispel his growing fear. He knew that he had kept the sun to his left side as the morning had turned into afternoon, which meant he should have been traveling straight down the canyon. Besides, the canyon was not that wide. He decide to be more cautious and just travel from landmark to landmark, picking out a tree, shrub, or rock and walking to it before sighting in on the next one. It seemed to be working until an hour later when he realized he had reached the same tree he had used as his first landmark.

Now his panic and desperation were growing, particularly since it would be getting dark in a few more hours, when the sun disappeared completely behind the canyon wall. Bob decided to rest for a few minutes and collect his thoughts; he knew there had to be a way out of this hellish place. He stretched out under the meager shade of a small pine tree and dozed off. A few minutes later, he awoke with a start. He suddenly knew exactly where he was; he had blundered into Penitente Canyon. He donned his pack and set off at a rapid pace, not worrying about landmarks or the position of the sun, just worrying about getting out of the canyon before darkness fell. Somewhere deep inside himself, he knew he would not survive a night in this deadly place.

Finally, he found himself at the northern entrance and to his relief saw Ponil Creek splashing its way down Ponil Canyon. For some reason Penitente had released its hold on him and he had made it out just as the sun was setting. He had been in the small canyon for nine hours.

TORTURED SOULS

According to legend, Penitente Canyon is named for an obscure and extinct Indian tribe, which practiced torture and human sacrifice as part of their religion. The Anasazi were believed to have tortured suspected witches and used corpse powder in some of their rituals, but what occurred in Penitente Canyon goes far beyond anything attributed to the "Ancient Ones." Nothing else seems to be known about this mysterious other tribe aside from the fact that they used the canyon as the location for their bloody rituals which began long before the Spanish set foot in the new world.

At one time during the period when Ponil was still the wrangler headquarters, one of the wranglers was riding near the northern entrance to Penitente when he heard horrible screams coming from inside the canyon. Since his horse immediately panicked and refused to go near the entrance, the cowboy dismounted and walked in on foot. He had only gone a few hundred yards when he found himself in the middle of a scene of indescribable carnage. He was a grizzled veteran of the range, and thought he had seen just about everything, but never anything like the horror assaulting his senses now. Tortured and mangled bodies were everywhere, hanging limply from trees, staked out on the ground and even tied to boulders.

This was truly a scene from hell thought the cowboy as he tried to compose himself. It seemed both real and unreal at the same time, as if he had crossed a threshold which mortal man was not meant to go beyond. There appeared to be no one alive, but he could not be sure. He fought the almost overwhelming urge to run and approached the body of one man, who had apparently been skinned alive. The man was hanging from the limb of a withered tree, which was bare of leaves. His copper skinned face was the only part of his body untouched and his eyes were frozen open in horror. He appeared to be barely more than a teenager. As the wrangler drew near, the body vanished, as did the others, and the cowboy found himself alone in the canyon.

This time he did turn and run, leaving the canyon as fast as his legs would carry him. He never returned, even though he knew now that what he had witnessed was just a haunting scene from Philmont's storied past, a scene that continues to personally haunt him to this day.

SIX

RAYADO

Rayado sits on the edge of Philmont property and is the site of the first permanent settlement established on the Beaubien-Miranda land grant. It was started by Lucien Maxwell in the late 1840s. Maxwell's original home is still there along with a trading post and stagecoach stop. The home of famous frontiersman Kit Carson, who resided in Rayado from 1849 to 1851, is now a museum run by Philmont staff members as the Kit Carson Museum.

A small church called the Holy Child Chapel sits across the road from the museum. This part of Philmont is a green and lush area near the Rayado River, which contains some of the nicest brown trout found in New Mexico. However, as is the case with most places on the ranch, the little community is home to some rather unique residents.

THE PIANO

In the spring of 1850 a couple we shall simply refer to as Kathleen and Troy, since their names have been lost to history, were very much in love and engaged to be married. Troy was a young sandy haired Lieutenant of Dragoons (mounted infantry) and had been assigned to the United States Army's 1st Dragoons stationed in Taos, New Mexico. For reasons known only to them, the couple, who had met in St. Louis, decided that Kathleen would leave for Taos ahead of her fiancé, while he would accompany a later wagon train. They would be married when they were both safely in Taos.

Troy knew well the hardships his bride-to-be would face on a frontier army post and decided that she would have at least one reminder of a more gentile way of life. For that purpose he purchased a baby box grand piano and had it carefully crated to accompany Kathleen in her wagon. The journey to New Mexico was filled with danger and hardship, but Kathleen, with her freckled face and fiery auburn hair was of sound Irish stock and took the trip in stride. She and her beloved engagement gift made it to Taos, only to find that Troy's company of dragoons had been transferred to a lonely outpost called Rayado.

Kathleen decided to continue her journey so that she could prepare whatever quarters they were assigned to for her fiancé's arrival. She made up her mind that they would just have to be married in Rayado, wherever that was. Upon her arrival in the lonely colony, the Maxwell and Carson families, who immediately took her in, greeted her warmly. The Kit Carson home is a large rectangular structure surrounding a sub-stantial courtyard. One entire side is devoted to a big room called the dance hall that served as a gathering place for the town's residents and wel-comed travelers. It was in the dance hall that Kathleen's piano was placed and she practiced on it daily while she waited for her soldier to ar-rive.

It was just after Christmas that year when word arrived that the young Lieutenant who was assigned to Company G of the 1st Dragoons had been killed along with many others when Comanches had attacked his wagon train. The pretty Irish colleen was devastated by the news and for a long time inconsolable. She remained at Rayado for several years and continued to play her piano every day, but the songs she played were no longer the lively tunes she had planned to delight Troy with; instead her delicate fingers played the sad and lonely Irish songs of a broken-hearted lover.

Kathleen eventually moved on, possibly back to Taos or even St. Louis. The piano remained, however, and was never sent for by the girl. It was finally put into storage since none of the other residents could play it. It stayed there for years, gathering dust until resurrected by Philmont staff members. It was moved back into the dance hall to be part of the Kit Carson Museum displays. Shortly thereafter the staff members residing in the compound began to be awakened at night by the sounds of sad songs being played on the baby box grand.

This is not a player piano; there are no scrolls of music. Yet, numerous visitors have entered the forlorn and otherwise empty dance hall in the darkness of night, drawn by the sounds of the haunting melodies. When they shine their flashlights or raise their oil lamps over the keyboard, they will see the keys being pressed down by unseen fingers. No one sits on the stool, yet the piano plays on. It can only be assumed that Kathleen has returned to play for the young dragoon whose arrival is still awaited at a place called Rayado.

THE LONELY BUGLER

When the army established its outpost at Rayado in early June of 1850, one of the soldiers in the detachment was a baby-faced bugler far from his home in the East. His name was Scotty Campbell. He was popular with his fellow soldiers, often entertaining them in the evening with the wide repertoire of tunes he could play on his shiny brass horn.

For Scotty this was the adventure of a lifetime. He had been orphaned when just a lad and forced to live with a sour maiden aunt. Now he had found a home in the army and he loved the New Mexico countryside, particularly Rayado, which was both beautiful and peaceful. It was hard for him to believe that there had been Indian trouble in the area and he felt sure that now that the dragoons had arrived the warriors had departed. Thus, Scotty committed the cardinal sin for a soldier; he wandered away from the outpost one day to explore the area, and he went unarmed.

About an hour later, the post was attacked by a large band of Apaches who drove off the herd of livestock belonging to Lucien Maxwell. The dragoons quickly mounted and set off in pursuit, painfully aware that their young bugler was missing. They found his body near the Rayado River; he had been pierced by half a dozen arrows, and his skull had been crushed. All of the troopers prayed that he had died before some of the other atrocities had been committed on his frail body. Two of the soldiers wrapped him gently in a blanket and took his body back to the Maxwell house, part of which had been set aside as an infirmary for the troops. There he was laid out on one of the bunks until the company could return and give him a proper burial.

The Maxwell house sits locked and abandoned now, not far from the Kit Carson Museum. The room which housed the infirmary has a large bay window facing south, and it was this window which a staff member named Bruce Williams was passing one day in the summer of 1994 while leading a string of burros. He saw what appeared to be the figure of a man looking out of the bay window. Knowing that the house was always kept locked, he tied off the burros and approached the window, concerned that someone had broken in. He was not the slightest bit afraid since the man appeared to be of small stature, and Bruce was a large athletic type who was sure he could handle any trouble.

As Bruce drew closer he could make out in the dimming evening light that the figure was dressed in a blue uniform of some kind. Then he saw the face, green and decaying and clearly the face of death. Any idea he had entertained of facing this challenge head on evaporated. Bruce retreated quickly, and only later that night did he secure enough courage to return with several other staff members. They found the house securely locked, but could view every room in the house by shining their flashlights through the numerous windows. They saw no one in any of the rooms and nothing appeared to have been disturbed. However, they returned the next day with a key and made another thorough search. They again found no one.

The lonely bugler has shown himself to other staff members and museum visitors on several occasions in the last few years. He is always standing at the bay window, looking to the south through eyes long past seeing in this mortal world. That's the direction his friends and fellow soldiers had taken in pursuit of the raiding Apache, and he obviously awaits their return, perhaps hoping that this time instead of burying his corpse in a grave which has long since disappeared, they will gather around and listen to him play his bugle.

Given the history of Philmont, I found myself turning from the window after I had heard this story and looking to the south, half expecting to see a column of men in blue coming over the rise. When they do come, and I believe that someday they will, it will be to take their young companion with them on their endless ride, where he will never have to be lonely again.

THE EAGLE IN THE WINDOW

When I initially approached the bay window of the Maxwell house to take some pictures I noticed something both bizarre yet strangely moving. One of the panes of glass was broken, yet it was a break like none I had ever seen before. It was in the perfect shape of an eagle in flight.

The eagle is a sacred symbol to the Boy Scouts of America, and the coveted rank of Eagle Scout is the highest a young man can attain. The break had not been noticed by anyone before and could not be explained. How it occurred will never be known, but it is certainly another one of those strange and wonderful sights, which captivate visitors to Philmont.

THE INNKEEPER

Shortly after Kit Carson returned to Taos to live, Lucien Maxwell moved his operation to Cimarron and left Rayado in the care of Jesus Abreu. Jesus constructed a trading post and stagecoach stop that were lucrative for quite a while. The original structure is still there and now houses a replica of the trading post, as well as, the Kit Carson Museum gift shop and living quarters for some of the museum staff. It also houses a colony of noisy bats, but they were not what was causing the disturbances which bothered Steve Benelli and his roommate in 1998.

They were housed in a room at the rear of the building directly across from the old storage room and next to the gift shop. Their only door opened up on the long covered porch, which divides the building in half. They would often return in the evening to find the upper half of their double door open despite the fact that they had secured it in the morning before taking up their jobs at the museum. In addition, they were constantly hearing footsteps at night, both in front of their room and in the gift shop next door. They made repeated attempts to catch the intruder, but to no avail since they never saw anyone and the gift shop was always found securely locked, as it had been when they retired.

The young men decided they were probably dealing with the ghost of Jesus Abreu, who is buried in a cemetery not far from the building, and they tried to ignore his nightly forays. However, he became noisier and noisier and began to rearrange items in both the gift shop and restored trading post. Occasional disturbances were now turning into sleepless nights and finally Steve's roommate, who is a holder of priesthood in the Mormon Church. could take no more. One late evening when the wayward spirit had been particularly active, the priest performed a formal blessing ceremony in the building.

After the ceremony, the building was quiet, and the staff members had no more problems. It is believed that either the blessing worked, or perhaps, just satisfied Jesus that his inn was safe. Unfortunately, the blessing had no effect on the bats, which continue their nightly forays from the attic, noisily reminding everyone that they are as much a part of the Philmont landscape as Baldy Mountain or Urraca Mesa.

SEVEN

THE FRENCH HENRY MINE

The French Henry mine is named after Henry Buruel, a Frenchman who secured gold mining rights from Lucien Maxwell. It is a favorite stop for crews hiking Philmont's north country. There is a mining museum to visit and campers can pan for gold in South Ponil Creek where good-sized nuggets are still occasionally found. Campers can also tour the second level of the famous Azteca mine and still find out for themselves how dark and dangerous gold mines really were around the turn of the century.

OLD JAKE

It is a tradition at Philmont that staff members at a staff camp dress in the authentic costumes of the people they represent, whether miners, cowboys, or mountain men. Several years ago, the staff at French Henry were going through some old pictures of the area and its inhabitants in order to better recreate their costumes. The cabin they were in is spacious and authentic. With no electricity or indoor plumbing; they worked until late at night by the light of their oil lanterns.

Later, after everyone had retired, one of the female staff members by the name of Jill awoke in her room in the cabin to see what appeared to be an old miner sitting in the rafters above her bunk. In the belief that she was only dreaming or letting her imagination get the better of her, she closed her eyes and attempted to shake off the image. However, when she opened her eyes again, he was still there. He was a short wiry little man with a graying and unkempt full beard and head of hair.

Now she was truly frightened and she pulled her sleeping bag up over her head, only to feel someone or something grab her ankles and began pulling her out of the bunk toward the cabin door. Her frantic screams alerted other staff members who reached her just as her feet were being dragged out of the front door.

Her friends quickly grabbed her shoulders and the ends of the sleeping bag around them. A fierce tug of war ensued with an unseen force that ended with Jill being finally extracted from the bag just as it was jerked completely out of the cabin. Although Jill was thoroughly banged up and bruised, she was otherwise physically all right. No one in the camp slept again that night. The next morning they decided to look through the pictures again and in one of them, Jill identified her attacker. A further investigation identified him only as Jake, a miner who had been killed in the late 1870s in one of the all too frequent mining accidents.

Although he has never been seen again or assaulted anyone else, the old miner's footsteps are often heard in and around the cabin at night. Objects on shelves often jump off by themselves, even in broad daylight, signifying Jake's continued presence. Just to be on the safe side, staff members set a place at the table for the old man at each meal.

EIGHT

CLARKS FORK

Clarks Fork is the Western Lore Camp for the central area of Philmont and was established in 1941. It features horseback riding, branding, a chuck wagon dinner, and a campfire program. There is no question that Clarks Fork is haunted; the only questions are whether there is more than one ghost, and who they might be. The summer of 1999, when I did most of the interviews for this book, seems to have been the most haunted summer in recent history for this particular camp.

THE GRAY RIDER

The ghost known only as the Gray Rider was first reported not long after Clarks Fork was opened as a staff camp. A group of new wranglers riding out from the camp one morning was surprised to see a lone cowboy on a nearby ridge watching them. His features were indistinguishable. He wore a long gray coat, a battered gray hat, and was sitting astride a large gray stallion. The wranglers ignored him at first even when they saw him sitting in the same spot on their return that evening.

However, when he appeared again the next morning, they decided to approach him to determine his identity. As they drew near, he abruptly vanished. He was seen virtually every day after that but would never speak or come any closer to the wranglers than the top of the ridge. These sightings have continued on a regular basis since that time, but in recent years the Gray Rider has become bolder and will sometimes ride right through the camp, appearing out of nowhere and disappearing just as quickly. He looks at no one, and any attempts to address him are ignored.

Research has led staff members to believe that the Gray Rider is the ghost of Zeb Clark who used to live in the area that bears his name and who often acted as a guide for hunting parties. While Zeb is always seen riding alone there have been some indications that he may on occasion be driving a phantom herd of horses.

One day in the summer of 1995 Will Billings, a tall, slender, red-headed wrangler from California was repairing a cattle gap near Clarks Fork when he heard what sounded like a herd of horses on the run. The area around the cattle gap was open and flat. While he could clearly hear them, he could see nothing, as was the case with the previously reported incident on Urraca Mesa. Will was not alone in hearing the distinctive sounds. He could tell by the reactions of the pinto he was riding that his horse heard them too and wanted no part of this invisible wild herd. It was all he could do to keep the pinto from bolting until the noise of the herd faded into the distance.

THE PRANKSTER

In recent years, either Zeb Clark has changed from being a simple old cowboy who wants to keep an eye on the strangers occupying the property to a mischievous prankster, or a new spirit has appeared at Clarks Fork. This newcomer has never been seen, but his nighttime antics play havoc with the wranglers' bunkhouse and the Program Counselor's cabin.

One night during the summer of 1999, the wranglers were expecting the return of Matt Pease, who had been enjoying a few days off. They heard the gate outside open and then footsteps on the front porch. Then, strangely, there was a knock on the door, which would not have been necessary from Matt. When the door was opened, there was no one there. Matt arrived much later and decided to sleep on the front porch of the Program Director's cabin rather than disturb his friends.

The very next night one of the female wranglers was fixing her hair when several shampoo bottles, a razor, and a bag of candy suddenly jumped off of the shelves and flew across the bathroom, crashing into the opposite wall and falling to the floor. She quickly retreated to another room and a subsequent examination of the bathroom showed no signs of the shelves being tampered with, they were still completely level.

A few days later, several of the staff members were sitting on the front porch of the cabin when a cow skull, which was firmly attached to a post by a nail and strong wire, suddenly flew off the post and into the front yard. There was no one close to the skull when it happened and certainly no wind strong enough to snap the wire. Only someone with immense strength could have ripped the skull from its mooring, and that someone remains unseen.

On another occasion, a wrangler was sleeping alone in the bunkhouse when he was awakened by the sounds of the bunkhouse door opening and the tread of heavy footsteps walking up to and stopping at the foot of his bunk. When he lit the lantern by his bed, the room was ominously empty. He decided to spend the rest of the night in another location.

If this is, in fact, a new entity, it has just decided to make its presence known, and one can only speculate as to who it is and what its purpose is. According to the staff I talked with, the jury is still out as to whether they are just dealing with a fun loving spirit, or one that will escalate its attempts to frighten people away from Clarks Fork. No one has left yet, but then this newcomer may just be getting started.

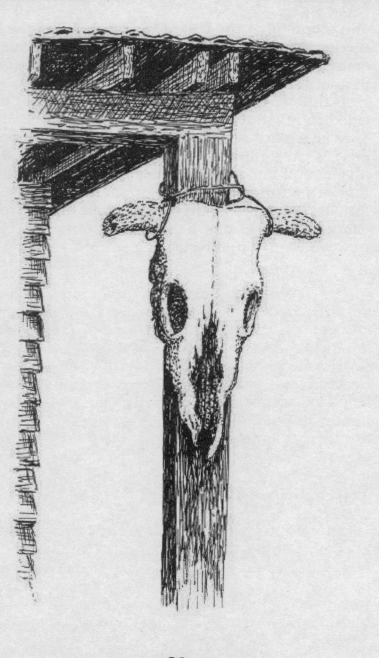

Nine

CYPHERS MINE

The area where Cyphers Mine is located was originally worked in the 1880s and is now a staff camp with a mining and gold panning program. In 1894, the original owners were bought out by the Colorado Consolidated Verde Mining and Milling Company. Charlie Cyphers was one of the managers of the company and he stubbornly refused to move on even when the company's mines completely played out. He continued to live in his cabin, which is still being used by the Philmont staff today, and search for gold. Even when Waite Phillips acquired the property, Charlie, who was known to old timers in Cimarron as an "old mountain goat", refused to leave until finally he just mysteriously disappeared one day.

Charlie's ghost is one of the most fascinating at Philmont since he can apparently change both his appearance and disposition. On one hand, he can be friendly and outgoing, and on the other, appear in a form designed to scare anyone senseless.

THE FRIENDLY SIDE OF CHARLIE

Impromptu jam sessions are frequent events in the evening at Philmont and the Cyphers Mine staff camp boasts of some of the best guitar players and banjo pickers on the ranch. This was a delight to a rookie staff member named Mark Conklin. He was a fair guitar player himself and loved to join in with the sessions that featured the music of a long gone era.

However, the stocky, fair-skinned lad was not enjoying what was happening to him every night after the lights went out. Upon first arriving at the camp, he had been shown a picture of the late Charlie Cyphers, which hung in the old man's cabin. Now Charlie was visiting him in his dreams every night, always wanting to know, in a not unfriendly fashion, "What's all this Boy Scout stuff was about?" It wasn't an overly frightening experience for Mark, but he was getting tired of having the same dream every night, which never failed to awaken him from a deep sleep.

Then one particularly beautiful New Mexico evening, the advisors were gathered on the porch of the staff cabin for the "advisors' coffee", a nightly ritual at staff camps which gives the adult crew members a few minutes away from their young charges. Naturally, the guitars and banjos were broken out and a particularly lively jam session started up featuring such songs as the "Philmont Hymn" and "Good Night Irene". As the music caressed the camp and surrounding trees, it was easy for both participants and listeners to drift back to a time when the world was less complicated.

At the end of a fine rendition of "Red River Valley", a man wearing a pair of well-worn overalls and a flannel work shirt approached the musicians from the end of the porch and complimented them on their "good playing". A big grin broke from his red beard and lit up his tanned face as he looked briefly into the eyes of each of the staff members. Then he turned, stepped off the porch and walked down the trail, vanishing into the first patch of forest.

Needless to say, the staff members were startled, none more so than Mark Conklin. They were startled and very shaken up, not because they had been complimented, but because the grizzled old man delivering the compliment had been none other than Charlie Cyphers himself.

Mark had no further dreams after Charlie's unexpected appearance that summer, so it can only be assumed that Charlie has decided that this "Boy Scout stuff" is all right after all. Unfortunately, that assumption offers no explanation for the form of certain other appearances by Charlie.

THE OTHER SIDE OF CHARLIE

Allegedly, after a standoff that lasted for several years, Charlie sold his mining claim to Waite Phillips for $100.00. However, rumors persist that Charlie never left his beloved mine, and that his disappearance had a much more sinister aspect. There were certainly men still roaming the mountains in those days who would not have hesitated to kill a lone miner just for the chance to search his belongings for any gold he might have stashed away. We will never know for sure if this is what happened to Charlie, but it is certainly suggested by an event that occurred sometime in the late 1980s.

Ralph Willis was one of the staff members who conducted tours of the mine that Charlie had worked so hard. After his last tour of the day, the blond good-looking college student headed back to staff headquarters. The trail took him by Charlie's old cabin that was used only as the site for the nightly "stomp", a good time program of music and dancing conducted each night for the campers. He was startled to hear a noise in the cabin like the sound of someone rummaging around in search of something.

Ralph knew there should be no one in the cabin this time of the day, and thinking that some camper had wandered inside, he climbed the creaky steps and opened the front door. To his surprise, he saw an adult, his back turned to Ralph, busily digging into a box of rusty old mining tools. Since the man was clearly dressed in 1920s mining attire, the veteran staff member thought he might just be a new staff member and asked politely if he could help him.

What he saw when the man turned around sent him reeling back out of the cabin and down the steps. The face was not that of a camper or a new staff member, but of someone long dead, his features contorted in a horrible grimace which was obviously due to the gaping wound across his throat which appeared clotted with dried blood.

Ralph ran to the staff cabin and breathlessly blurted out his story. He was met with initial derision and disbelief until the camp director, another long time Philmont veteran, quieted the other staff members by admitting that he had seen the same apparition several summers before. Ralph was therefore not the first to see this side of Charlie Cyphers; nor was he the last since several more sightings have been reported since then.

It is now believed by many that Charlie was murdered and that his ghost returns in this form in search of either his stolen gold or perhaps his killer. Either way, he is one of those things that go bump in the night that no one particularly cares to meet, at least not in that form.

TEN

DAN BEARD

Dan Beard Camp is a staff camp located in Philmont's North Country. It is named after Daniel Carter Beard, one of the men who helped found the Boy Scout movement in the United States. It is the home of challenge events. These are a group of difficult problems designed to test scout crews both mentally and physically, and to impress upon them the necessity of working together as a team.

There is apparently another challenge at Dan Beard too; only this one presents a challenge to the imagination and to one's belief in the world of spirits.

THE HIKER

Ben Vargas has been the horse foreman at Philmont for a number of years and likes to hunt the plentiful game on the ranch during the fall and winter. Several years ago, he took an elderly friend hunting for elk up around Dan Beard. The altitude can take its toll on even the most fit and the older man quickly tired, so when they arrived at the camp Ben pulled a chair out of the staff cabin and took it to an outbuilding where the two men had decided to sit and wait for the elk to come in at dusk. It was a cloudy day, but not particularly cold for that time of year so there was no reason for the animals not to be on the move. It was just a matter of waiting.

About 4:00 o'clock in the afternoon, Ben's guest was sitting comfortably behind the door of the building when Ben got up to look around. Suddenly, a gust of icy cold wind came from nowhere and blew through the cabin door causing the old man to put his head down and begin shivering. Ben had just turned to take care of him when he glanced back through the door and saw someone walking across the meadow in front of the building. The man appeared to be middle aged and was wearing the traditional Boy Scout campaign hat, often referred to as a "Smoky the Bear" hat, wire rimmed glasses, and a heavy coat.

At first Ben was just curious because no one else was authorized to be in the area during this time of year. The stranger looked up, saw Ben, and nodded his head in the horse foreman's direction. Ben returned the greeting and the man took three or four more steps and simply vanished. Ben has no idea who the stranger was, and never saw him again.

However, seeing a ghostly figure of this type on a Philmont trail should not be that unexpected. While the staff works very hard to make sure it is a safe place for campers, there are still inherent dangers in a wilderness environment that requires strenuous hiking and climbing. There are some injuries every summer and an occasional death, most often that of an adult advisor who has a heart attack while on the trail. It would therefore not be surprising to see the spirit of a middle-aged scout leader who died on the trail, but refuses to leave until he finishes his trek.

On the other hand, perhaps Ben ran into the ghost of Dan Carter Beard himself, who prefers to remain in "God's Country" enjoying the sight of so many young people experiencing a once in a lifetime adventure in a program he helped found.

Eleven

THE SPANISH LADY

Located one-half mile from the Philmont base camp is the wrangler headquarters, where the full and part-time wranglers do the difficult work of preparing the horses for the summer activities. Their effort starts in mid-May well before the first crews arrive and consist of shoeing the horses and breaking in the new mounts.

Ben Vargas and his family live in a house provided for them right at the entrance to the road leading to the bunkhouse, corrals and stables. Ben is slim and wiry and has been a cowboy all of his life as were his father and grandfather before him. He knows horses as well as anyone, but he does not know much about ghosts, even though he apparently lives with one he has never seen.

The house itself is not particularly large but it is adequate for Ben and his family. There is a beautiful view of the mountains that rise majestically on the Philmont property and tower over both the base camp and the wrangler headquarters. Even late into the summer one can sometimes still see patches of snow on the larger peaks. It is obvious that this view is what has attracted people to the Philmont area and perhaps keeps many of them there long after they should be gone.

According to Jake Anderson, one of the Philmont wranglers, he was driving past Ben's house one day when he saw an elderly Spanish woman sitting on the steps of the house. She was dressed in a white flannel nightgown and she merrily returned Jake's wave. Later that evening, the cowboy asked Ben who the lady was that was staying at his home. Ben was obviously puzzled since he said no one was staying with them and they had had no visitors all day. He was even more puzzled when the lady was described to him for neither he nor his wife knew anyone who fitted that description, and wrangler headquarters is too far away from town for someone, particularly an elderly woman, to just wander into.

The mystery has never been solved, but it is quite possible that Jake encountered the ghost of one of the Abreu women, for this area had been their domain for many years. They were a combination of hardy pioneer women and true Spanish ladies who had settled in and around Rayado. Most of them are buried with their husbands, fathers and sons on the Philmont property, and there is no reason to think that they do not return on occasion, just to sit on the steps and admire the view of their mountains.

TWELVE

THE CIMARRON WITCH

The town of Cimarron is a small community of about seven hundred people which doubles in size when the full Philmont staff comes in every summer. It is a pretty little town and an old one. The Wild West heritage is evident from the solidly built old buildings to the occasional herd of cattle or horses being driven through the main street. Cimarron's residents are typical of New Mexico, both friendly and easygoing. They take care of their own, but warmly welcome strangers into their midst. Overall it's an unlikely place to find a witch. Yet, according to old timers, Cimarron had its very own resident witch for several years.

She lived in a broken down shack on the outskirts of town, and no one knew for sure where she came from, or where she got the few dollars she spent to survive. Of course, most people were not sure they really wanted to know. Her appearance was not overly startling, except for her tendency to wear outlandish costumes usually made up of a combination of Native American, Hispanic, and 1960s hippie castoff clothing. She was short in stature and so thin as to appear almost anorexic so this clothing always seemed to be two sizes too large for her.

Her ancestry was as confusing as her clothing. She sported a mane of unkempt black hair, light green eyes, and dark skin. The town's citizens often argued over the question of whether she was Apache, Hispanic, or Anglo, or a combination of all three. However, she was not what one would call ugly, as witches are often characterized, and she definitely had no warts on her rather prominent nose.

There was just something vaguely sinister about her. People gave her a wide birth when she roamed aimlessly through the town, an event that occurred on an almost daily basis. It was probably the local teenagers who first labeled her a witch, and they too avoided her with the exception of two brothers we shall call Mike and Carl. They were the teenage sons of one of the full time Philmont wranglers at Ponil, and they would go out of their way to tease the "witch" when they crossed her path in town.

They were not really cruel, more mischievous; openly calling her a witch to her face and demanding that she give them magic spells or potions to attract girls or money. She generally ignored their taunting until one crisp October day when they apparently went too far. No one knows what was said but witnesses said her green eyes turned dark and flashed with anger. She said nothing, but raised one slender arm and pointed her finger menacingly at the two boys. For their part, they decided a strategic withdrawal was definitely in order, and they made a hasty retreat to their beat-up 1962 Chevy pick up. With their trademark squealing of tires and cloud of dust, they left town heading for Ponil.

Mike was driving and clearly nervous. He was going way too fast on the gravel road. Suddenly, an enormous owl appeared in front of the truck. It was the biggest bird either of the boys had ever seen and it had a huge wingspan, large enough to cover the vehicle's windshield and block their view when it settled on the hood. Mike immediately lost control and the truck slid wildly off the gravel road into some scrub brush. Neither boy was hurt, but the owl was not finished with them yet. It kept crashing its enormous body into the windshield until the glass cracked.

Carl was the first to recover his senses and react. He grabbed his 30.06 rifle off the rack on the back window and slid out the passenger door managing to get off several shots before the owl flew away. The first shot missed wildly, but the second round caused feathers to fly off the bird's left wing. Carl knew he had scored a hit. However, the strange bird just continued to fly away and disappeared over the horizon.

The two teenagers were unnerved by what had happened to them, but since no real harm had been done, they quickly dismissed it from their minds. At least that was the case until two days later when they made a trip into town and saw the witch. She was sporting a crude bandage on her left arm and it was in a sling. The boys did not even think about asking her what had happened, especially once she gave them an enigmatic smile when she saw them. They just made sure from that day forward to treat her with the utmost respect and caution.

THIRTEEN

THE SANTA FE TRAIL

The Santa Fe Trail is one of the most famous of the western trails. It was established in 1821 by an expedition led by Captain William Becknell who sought to set up a trade route between Missouri and Mexico, which had recently won its independence from Spain. The trail was used primarily for commerce until New Mexico was acquired by the United States and then more and more pioneer families found the trail to be the best route to new homesteads in the Southwest.

The Santa Fe Trail was harsh and dangerous. There were marauding Indian bands to deal with, as well as the weather that ran the gamut from searing heat to numbing cold. The route wound its way through Philmont and parts of it can still be clearly seen from the Tooth of Time, an outcrop of rock on a ridge that overlooks the Philmont base camp and provides some of the most spectacular views on the ranch.

Broken pieces of old wagons or other artifacts of the struggle along the trail are still occasionally found, but it is at night that the trail seems to come back to life. Rangers hiking near the old route after dark will sometimes hear the creaking of wagon wheels or the colorful language of a teamster exhorting some stubborn mules to move along. It is also reported that if you happen to be with one of the hardy crews who climb the Tooth early in the morning to watch the spectacular sunrise, you may see the ghostly vision of a struggling wagon train moving along the trail in the dawning light. It is a vision that disappears with the rising of the sun.

These sightings tend to be benign, but sometimes someone will get closer to history than they really want to be.

THE ATTACK

Michelle Shepherd and Andrea Johnson were backcountry staff members who were heading back to their jobs after a couple of days off. It was close to midnight and the overcast sky eliminated any natural light as they neared the Old Santa Fe Trail. It was cold and forebodingly quiet when suddenly Michelle, a petite brunette from Mississippi heard what sounded like anxious voices off to her left. She reached out and grabbed the arm of her taller ebony companion. Before she could say anything, there was a scream and the night was lit up by the flashes of gunfire.

Both girls hit the ground shocked and dismayed that anyone could be so careless as to be shooting randomly on the ranch, particularly after dark. Then they both heard another ominous sound, that of horses crashing through the brush behind them. They turned to look just in time to see the vague, but unmistakable shapes of three mounted Indian warriors driving their mounts furiously toward the sounds of the firing.

They could not see the actual battle, which was too far away, but they could hear the sounds of a fight to the death including the war cries of the Indians, the curses of the white men, and worst of all, the screams of the dying. To the terrified young women hugging the ground, the battle seemed to last forever but actually was over very quickly. The menacing sounds died away and silence returned to Philmont and the Santa Fe Trail as Michelle and Andrea cautiously got to their feet and approached the battle site.

In the beams of the flashlight, they saw nothing but rocks, scrub brush and the old wagon ruts of the long abandoned trail. Then Michelle's right foot caught on something. She shined her light down and saw protruding from the packed earth the rusty barrel of an old rifle, the last remains of a long ago fight which both sides are doomed to replay in the darkness of New Mexico summer nights.

The two young women emerged from their experience unscathed but thereafter made sure that their hikes along the Santa Fe Trail occurred in the daylight when the spirits who inhabit the historic route appear to rest and regroup for their nightly forays into the world of the living.

FOURTEEN

THE TOOTH OF TIME

The climb to the top of the Tooth of Time is rugged and dangerous and only the most fit and experienced hikers should even attempt it. However, the view is worth the effort and like the crest of Baldy Mountain, it is one of the rites of passage for those coming to Philmont. Consequently, most campers who hike the Philmont South and Central country areas make the ascent, and as a result, there have been some serious injuries and several deaths over the years. The fact is, if you fall off of the tip of the Tooth you will plummet several hundred feet before hitting the rocky ground below and there is virtually no chance of survival.

THE RANGER TRAINEE

According to Karl Schmidt, a Philmont ranger, such a tragedy happened in 1996 when a young female ranger trainee fell from the Tooth and was killed. It occurred at the beginning of the summer when the rookie rangers were being shown the ropes on special training hikes which would get them prepared both mentally and physically to lead the crews of campers scheduled to begin arriving shortly.

The trainee, whom we shall call Marie, was a lively nineteen-year-old with an outgoing personality and good sense of humor which served her well since at 5'4" with a slightly built frame, she was having a tough time with some of the physical challenges. However, she met them well and was considered to be among the most promising of the rookies.

Her training crew was under the capable hands of several veteran rangers and they had gotten their charges up at 3:00 a.m. so they could ascend Tooth Ridge and climb the Tooth in time to see the awesome rising of the sun over the Philmont landscape. The crew made it to the top with no problem and was just settling in to await sunrise when the predawn stillness was shattered by a horrifying scream.

No one actually saw Marie fall so it will never be known exactly what happened, but apparently she wandered too close to the edge and lost her footing. When the other members of her crew reached her broken body, in addition to the other injuries, they saw that her fingernails were all torn away, indications of the frantic efforts she made to stop her fall by grabbing at the rocky outcrop as she slipped off.

None of those present that day will ever forget the sight of their companion lying in a heap at the base of the ridge, nor will they forget the sound of her screaming as she fell to her death. According to Karl and many others, these screams can still be heard today by crews who visit the Tooth in the early morning hours, near the time of her fall.

Even more unnerving is the sight that has greeted some campers as they reach the top of the tooth. There before them in the dim light is the figure of a young woman in a torn and tattered green ranger shirt, her body and face covered in blood. She is roaming around the granite promenade as if searching for something. She never seems to find the object of her quest, but will disappear before their very eyes after a few moments.

Perhaps she is still trying to find the one hand-hold that will break her fall, or perhaps she just refuses to accept what happened to her. In either case, she is the loneliest and one of the most heart-wrenching of the Philmont ghosts.

FIFTEEN

THE ST. JAMES HOTEL

No book about Philmont ghosts would be complete without a chapter devoted to the St. James Hotel in Cimarron. The hotel is a two-story adobe-like structure near the Cimarron River. It was built in 1872 by Henri Lambert, who had been a chef for President Abraham Lincoln. Because of its outstanding cuisine and lively saloon, it soon became a mecca for anyone traveling in the area. The old guest register is still on display in the lobby and includes such famous, and infamous, names as Buffalo Bill Cody, Bat Masterson, Annie Oakley, Zane Grey, and a Mr. Howard, favorite alias of Jesse James.

It was also a favorite watering hole for Clay Allison, a notorious gunfighter who figured prominently in the Colfax County land war. It is a known fact that twenty-six men were killed in gunfights in the St. James saloon, several by Allison, and numerous bullet holes are still visible in the ceiling of what is now the hotel dining room. While some more modern rooms have been added to the hotel over the years, the original structure still stands and guests can stay in the same rooms where Jesse James and Annie Oakley once spent the night.

Due to its reputation for housing numerous things that go bump in the night, the St. James has been featured on television's "Unsolved Mysteries". There are at least four ghosts in residence that the staff knows of; however, considering the frequency of the manifestations, it is impossible to know for sure how many are roaming the halls. One thing is certain, this unusual influx of paranormal activity makes it difficult to keep a full hotel staff, and my hat is off to those hardy few like Rebekah Ellis and Pat Gruver who seem to consider encounters with the long dead all part of a day's work at the St. James.

THE ROSE LADY

Mary Lambert was the wife of the hotel's founder Henri, and continued to live in Room 17 of the hotel after he died, and until her death some years later. She was, by most accounts a delightful little lady. According to staff and guests, she still considers the hotel her home and roams about at will. She does not appreciate changes to the hotel and becomes more active and somewhat feisty when renovations are being undertaken.

It is not at all unusual for guests staying in Room 17 to wake up in the middle of the night and see Mary standing at the foot of their bed, or rocking in her chair. The chair rocks frequently by itself, and apparently only those who Mary decided she particularly likes get to actually see her.

Rebekah Ellis was working in the hotel in the summer of 1999 when I made my most recent of my five visits. She informed me that several weeks into the summer she was conducting a tour of the hotel for two female tourists. She invited them to see Mary's room which is upstairs and which Rebekah had never been in, up to that time. Upon entering the room and nearing the bed, she could smell a distinctive perfume with the fragrance of roses. There were no roses in the room and when she moved away from the bed the odor disappeared. She invited the two guests to stand by the bed, and they too could smell the perfume. She knew then that they had encountered Mary's spirit for that was the scent she constantly wore. Sightings of her are often preceded by the fragrance.

Pat Gruver has been the manager of the St. James for the last three years. This is her second time working at the hotel, and she reports actually seeing Mary twice and feeling her presence on many other occasions. She has seen Mary standing at the top of the stairs leading to the second floor and has seen her in her room. Her most recent encounter occurred in the summer of 1999 just several weeks before my visit. She was showing Room 17 to a young couple and was explaining that Mary's presence is often preceded by a sudden and significant lowering of the temperature in the room, an eerie sensation which will literally cause one's hair to stand up, and finally, the aroma of her rose perfume.

Just as Pat finished her explanation, the manifestations she had talked about all began to occur; and suddenly Mary appeared, gliding effortlessly between Pat and the young man. Everyone saw her clearly. A few days later Mary appeared again to a couple occupying the room. She used one of her favorite tricks, waking them up by standing at the foot of the bed, staring at them until they became aware of her presence. She has also been seen recently by guests in the Jesse James Room and Room 11.

Mary can also be fussy about how her room is kept. It must be exactly right, and her sheets must be spotlessly clean. Each room in the hotel has its distinctive set of linens, and the housekeepers have reported on several occasions that after washing the sheets they will pack them all up, including Mary's, and take them upstairs to the guest rooms. However, when they get to Mary's room, her sheets will be missing and are usually found back downstairs, probably indicating that Mary is not satisfied with their cleanliness. If the sheets are rewashed, she is usually satisfied.

The ghost of Mary Lambert seems to be perfectly content in her existence, and will continue to watch over the hotel and its guests as long as the St. James stands.

THE COWBOY

While Mary Lambert is certainly well known around the St. James, she is not the most famous of the ghostly residents. That honor is reserved for T.J. Wright, a cowboy who worked for one of the larger ranches near Cimarron. One night many years ago after Henri Lambert was long dead, T.J. Wright won the hotel in a poker game with the latest owner. When he came to town the next morning to claim his winnings, he was shot down right outside of the hotel by an unknown assailant. He was taken into the building and upstairs to Room 18 where he died two days later.

Since T.J.'s death, any attempts to rent out Room 18 have met with disaster. T.J.'s ghost will roam the hallways in protest, showing his displeasure by breaking vases, light fixtures and crockery. Owners of the hotel decided long ago that T.J. still believes the place to be his, fairly won, and it is best to keep him happy by keeping Room 18 locked and unavailable to guests. However, T.J., being the rambunctious cowboy that he is, requires more than just his privacy.

The hotel staff has also found it necessary to change his linens every month and to place a fresh bottle of Jack Daniels whisky in the room every few weeks since T.J. apparently still has a taste for good liquor, although sometimes it seems to get the best of him. Rebekah Ellis told me that on one occasion they opened the lobby early in the morning to find a guest ready to check out. When asked how his stay had been, he responded by inquiring if Room 18 had been rented the night before. When they told him it had not been, he seemed puzzled and told Rebekah and Pat that he had been awakened several times during the night by loud noises in Room 18 which was right next door to him. The staff thought it wise not to go into details about what he had probably heard.

T.J. also likes to have his room aired out occasionally. The door to each guest room in the hotel is topped by a beautiful hand painted transom that can only be unlocked and opened from inside the room. The one above T.J.'s door frequently opens and closes by itself. On one recent day the room must have been particularly stuffy for the old cowboy because despite the fact that it was locked as usual, the door flew open violently, scaring two of the housekeepers upstairs at the time so badly that they both rushed downstairs and quit their jobs.

Unfortunately, T.J. can get down right mean at times, if he considers his privacy to be seriously violated. Patricia R. Lotee, a former owner of the hotel in the 1980s wrote a pamphlet about the hotel entitled "St. James Hotel, the 'SPECIAL PLACE'. She tells of her first visit to Room 18 when she encountered a "spiral, swirling, milk white something" in the corner of the room which attacked her several times, driving her to her knees and forcing her to back out of the room. She also wrote that T.J. would often manifest himself as a chilling cold spot, which he did when the camera crew from "Unsolved Mysteries" was filming at the hotel.

There was another incident when a group of middle school students was being given a tour of the hotel by Pat Gruver. She took them upstairs in small groups accompanied by their teacher and they were cautioned to be quiet and respectful. Instead, they began pounding on the door of Room 18 and shouting. As a result, they were taken downstairs and a second group was brought up, but they did the same thing. By the time the third and final group got to the door and repeated the same unruly behavior, T.J. had had enough. As the students stood in front of the locked door there was a loud banging from inside the room and the door seemed ready to blow off its hinges. Pat said she and the teacher beat the kids down the stairs.

As I stood in front of the door to Room 18 and snapped several pictures, I was careful not to disturb the cranky old cowboy. After all, it is his hotel, assuming the hand that won it was fairly dealt, and whoever shot him certainly underestimated T.J.'s stubbornness. A debt is a debt, and T.J. Wright has certainly collected on this one.

THE LITTLE BOY

For many years, there was a corral and livery stable across the street from the St. James. There was a five-year-old boy whose father worked at the stable; and the boy was fond of playing around both the corral and the hotel. No one at the hotel seemed to mind since he was a delightful child with curly dark brown hair and green eyes that sparkled with mischief. It broke everyone's heart when one summer morning he was found drowned in the nearby Cimarron River.

However, he continues to play in the hotel, often seen by waitresses in the dining room who observe him sneaking around and taking great delight in rearranging the carefully laid out napkins and tablecloths. When spotted he disappears, leaving the echo of childish giggles behind him. Sometimes he chooses not to appear at all, but the hotel staff and guests will hear the unmistakable sounds of little feet running through the hotel. Long after his death, the lad continues his games in a place he loves.

THE IMP

In addition to the little fellow who drowned in the Cimarron River, there is another diminutive spirit who inhabits the hotel and is very active and mischievous. He has been around for over sixty years, yet no one has any idea of his origin; he is simply referred to as the "Imp". When seen, he initially appears to be about six-years-old, until one sees his face, which, while always smiling, is pock marked and aged like that of a much older man.

He has been seen all over the hotel, but his favorite spots for getting into trouble seem to be the kitchen and the gift shop. In 1993, while staying at the hotel with my family, I talked a great deal to the middle-aged woman who ran the gift shop, and she stated that the two biggest problems she had with the Imp were his affinity for stealing pens and his delight in playing with the door.

The shop manager told me that she could not keep pens in the shop because the minute she would lay one down and take her eyes off it even for a moment, it would disappear. Even when she attached a pen to one of her pockets she would often find it gone when she reached for it. However, the little thief does appear to have a good side. After a few weeks of losing pen after pen, my informant stated that she would open up the shop only to find all of the missing pens lined up neatly on the counter. Unfortunately, once she puts them in a drawer and starts taking them out one at a time for her use, the game begins again, as the pens disappear, one after another.

Visitors to the hotel know that the gift shop is open for business when the door is open, but the imp will frequently close it, sometimes right in the face of a guest. He never lets himself be seen when he pulls this stunt, preferring to remain anonymous, but everyone in the hotel is sure it is he.

They are just as sure that it is the Imp who delights in opening the ice machine and flinging scoops of ice at the waitresses and other kitchen staff. One waitress told me in 1993 that she had actually stood and watched the machine open and the scoop come out by itself before fleeing from the kitchen as the ice hit her in the back. This same waitress said that she and other waitresses also have their pens stolen from them, often disappearing from their own pockets, only to reappear several days later in the same pocket of their aprons, or even more bothersome, drop out of the sky and bounce off their heads.

The Imp is also credited with being the perpetrator of other pranks, such as switching lights on and off and causing the in-house telephone to ring when no one is on the line. Visitors to the hotel should also be warned not to be too surprised should they be sitting at the bar only to look up and see a little man with long white hair parked at the other end enjoying a beer. Actually, he is usually caught helping himself to the beer in the early morning hours, but who knows when he might just decide to join the gang one evening.

There is so much ghostly activity at the St. James that it is hard to keep up with what the various spirits are up to. I, for one, have begun to suspect the existence of an additional spirit, as yet unseen, who may be inhabiting the old hotel. His name was Charles Kennedy and his story may be the strangest of them all.

THE HEAD OF CHARLES KENNEDY

Colfax County certainly had more than its share of notorious outlaws and gunfighters, yet none was more notorious than Charles Kennedy, a huge, barrel-chested man with a scarred face. Charlie owned a small plot of land in the Moreno Valley, in the late 1880s, not far from Elizabethtown. He lived there in a spacious cabin with his Ute Indian wife and her young son.

Charlie was never one to do an honest days work if he could avoid it, so he developed the bad habit of enticing strangers traveling through the valley to spend the night at his cabin where, they were told, for a modest price they could get a fabulous meal and a bed for the night. Once the unsuspecting travelers were seated at the table in the cabin's main room, Charlie would come up behind them and either bludgeon them to death or put a bullet through their skull, both methods leaving a messy clean up job for his wife.

Then he would help himself to all of the belongings of the newly departed and store the bodies in the cellar until he had a chance to bury them in the garden. He is alleged to have done away with more than forty people in this manner. It is also said that he had a magnificent garden.

Charlie's demise came about when he left a body in the cellar a little too long and his stepson made the mistake of commenting about the foul odor in front of a newly arrived "guest". The man was a whiskey drummer, who, upon realizing what the odor was, politely excused himself and fled from the cabin. The innkeeper was so used to having his prey sitting quietly with their backs turned to him that the sight of the fleeing man completely froze him and the gentlemen got away unscathed. Charlie became so enraged that he picked his small stepson up by the feet and swung him against the stone fireplace, smashing his head to a bloody mess.

The boy's Ute mother was distraught, but too afraid of Kennedy to do anything about this latest atrocity until several months later on a snowy night when Charlie was drunk and passed out on the table. She sneaked out of the cabin and made her way to Elizabethtown, where she stumbled, half frozen, into a saloon where Clay Allison and a number of local miners and cowboys were hanging out. She blurted out her story to the astonished assemblage, who quickly decided that something must be done immediately.

It is interesting that the posse that captured Kennedy and placed him in the Elizabethtown jail was led by the outlaw, Clay Allison, who was probably indignant over the fact that another bad man was infringing on his territory. The posse had not bothered to dig up all of the bodies in the Kennedy garden; the ground was much too hard for that much labor. They did uncover enough to satisfy themselves that the squaw's story was true.

Once they had the madman safely tucked away however, the mob was outraged to learn that it would be months before a circuit judge made it to town to try the mass murderer. So, Allison and his cohorts, righteous citizens all, removed Charlie from the jail and took him to the local stockyard where they appointed their own judge, prosecutor, defense attorney, and jury and promptly held a trial. Needless to say, the hapless Charlie was found guilty and sentenced to hang, a sentence that was carried out forthwith on a handy scaffold used in the butchering of cattle.

Charlie did not die easily, fighting and cursing his captors as they threw him on a horse and slipped the noose around his thick neck. Of course, his neck failed to snap cleanly when the horse was driven from under him and witnesses reported that it took what seemed like hours for him to choke to death. When he was finally pronounced dead, Clay Allison had Kennedy's head removed and carried it with him to Cimarron. Here, it is said, he tried to persuade Henri Lambert to place the head in a jar and display it behind the bar in the St. James as a warning to others that such outrages as Charlie had committed would not be tolerated in Colfax County, New Mexico. Lambert was somewhat less than enthusiastic about the proposal, suspecting that the sight of a severed head embalmed in alcohol and floating in front of customers might be bad for business, but Clay Allison was not a person to whom one easily said no. The two men finally compromised and the head was displayed on a post of the hotel's corral. The head quickly mummified in the desert air, but after six months mysteriously disappeared from its perch.

This was not the end of the story however, since at the same time Kennedy's head had been removed, his heart had also been cut out and thrown on the porch of an Elizabethtown saloon to be food for the town's mongrel dogs. The dogs proved to be much more discriminating than expected and refused to touch the heart or go anywhere near it. It finally shriveled up and turned to dust.

No one has ever determined who stole Charles Kennedy's head, or what they did with it. It is certainly possible that some of the goings on in the St. James Hotel. The switching on of lights in vacant rooms and the opening and closing of doors at all times of the day and night can be attributed to Charlie's ghost searching in vain for his missing body parts. After all, as crowded as the St. James is with restless spirits, Charlie's ghost would probably feel right at home.

The problem for the hotel staff however, is what to do if it ever reaches the point where the ghosts out number the guests. After all, I suspect that it will be very hard to evict someone from a mere hotel when that person has already been evicted from life, yet still hangs around.

SIXTEEN

THE FACE IN THE PORTRAIT

The one thing you can be certain of when visiting Colfax County, New Mexico is that you need to be prepared for the unexpected. As I was conducting interviews and collecting the stories for this volume, I did not expect to uncover any hard proof of the existence of any of the ghosts. However, that is exactly what appears to have happened at the St. James.

I had completed my interview with Pat, the manager, and secured her permission to take pictures of the hotel. I, of course, took photographs of the door to Room 18, the inside of Mary Lambert's room and the dining room. I also took a picture of the hotel lobby, which includes a full-size portrait of Don Diego de Vargas, a famous Spanish missionary who spent many years trying to covert the Indian tribes to Christianity. When I arrived back home to Baton Rouge and had the pictures developed, I noticed something strange about the portrait; there appeared to be a face looking over the shoulder of Don Diego.

I immediately called Pat to ask about the portrait and was told that other than a mission in the background, and two figures of Apache Indians in the background near the bottom of the portrait, there was nothing else in the portrait. I had the photograph enlarged and have shown it to scores of people. Everyone agrees; they clearly see a face superimposed over the old mission. It is the face of a man, his mouth open in a silent scream.

Perhaps it is the face of T.J. Wright, letting us know in his usual mild mannered way that this is still his hotel. Or perhaps it is the head of Charles Kennedy, protesting his treatment at the hands of the mob and still trying to be reunited with his body. Either way it has provided a totally unexpected, and somewhat frightening exclamation point to this book, and also served as a reminder that the ghosts of Philmont are always out there. They wait patiently for the coming of summer and a new influx of staff and campers who will be both frightened and intrigued by their visit to a beautiful area where history is truly still very much alive.

EPILOGUE

I had thought this book finished when I wrote the chapter about the face in the portrait, however that was not to be the case. We have apparently stirred up at least one of the spirits associated with Philmont who has followed us back to Baton Rouge.

I asked Russ Roper, one of my former assistant scoutmasters and an outstanding artist, who teaches at a local Baton Rouge High School, to illustrate the book for me. He readily agreed to do so and had no problems until he was sitting alone in his classroom one afternoon doing the drawing of the door to Room 18 in the St. James. Suddenly, a portrait on the wall behind him flew off the wall and went right past his head. He found the event to be slightly disconcerting to say the least.

He was finishing up the drawing several nights later at his home when he took a break to get some Christmas decorations out of the attic. The whole family was shaken when a light fixture suddenly fell from the ceiling and shattered at Russ's feet.

It was shortly thereafter when I was sitting at my computer making some minor revisions on the chapter about the St. James Hotel that the first manifestations occurred in my home. It was quite late and my wife had already gone to bed, so the house was quiet. Suddenly, there were two loud knocks on the wall behind me. I knew the knocks had been on the wall, but I checked the doors anyway, and found no one outside. I was about to sit down at the computer again, when I heard a bedroom door upstairs open and close and the sound of footsteps in the hallway.

I was seriously concerned at this point since our children have all moved out of the house, and the upstairs is empty. I searched the house thoroughly this time and found no one. We now hear the footsteps and the opening of doors almost daily.

In addition, though no one in the house smokes cigarettes, our youngest daughter, Nicole, smelled cigarette smoke in her upstairs room several times when she was home from college for the holidays. Our new friend never really disturbed her although she did hear footsteps go by her room several times while she was home, and no one else was upstairs.

My wife, Kay and I live in a large home with three bedrooms upstairs and our large master bedroom at the foot of the stairs. We have a television set in our room and two comfortable chairs in front of it. From her chair, Kay can see the entire downstairs hallway reflected in the mirror of our dresser, which sits next to the TV set.

One Saturday night as we sat watching an old movie, we were both startled to hear footsteps coming down the stairs. There was no one else in the house so my wife automatically looked in the mirror and saw the shadowy figure of a tall, slim man reach the foot of the stairs and walk down the hallway toward the kitchen. I checked the house but found only our cocker spaniel that was extremely agitated at something in the kitchen that I could not see.

Riders in the Sky

It was not the first time our dog, Lady, has acted this way. She has frequently disturbed us in the middle of the night by standing at the base of the stairs and looking up while barking furiously. She will not, however, go up the stairs unless someone accompanies her.

Since the first startling confrontation, my wife has seen our visitor in the hallway at least a dozen times, and we have become quite used to his wanderings. Even the dog ignores him now. We call him T.J. since his appearance coincided with the work on T.J.'s picture and chapter, however, it could be any one of the Philmont spirits checking to see how the book is coming.

I hope he is pleased with the outcome.

ACKNOWLEDGMENTS

I have enjoyed working on this book more than any other piece I have ever done and a great deal of that is due to the help provided to me by both current and former Philmont staff members, as well as others who have contributed their time and talents to its preparation.

Thanks first to the adult staff at Philmont, George W. "Bill" Spice, the general manager, who allowed me to roam the ranch gathering material and Ben Vargas and Steve Zimmer for their contributions of stories and history.

Most of the stories came from the young summer staff members, who gave of their scarce time off to help me compile the various stories and legends, or wrote to me with their tales. These include, Matthew Vogel, Blake Tatum, Jake Anderson, Josh Houser, Steve Benelli, Mark Cadle, Matthew Pease, Jim Kachmar, Karl Schmidt, Michael Sawyer, Jeff Larsen, Luke Teske, and Kyle Gadley.

A special thanks goes to Pat Gruver, manager of the St. James Hotel, Rebekah Ellis, a St. James employee, and Buddy Morse of the Old Mill Museum.

Also, as the reader can see, Russ Roper did a wonderful job with the illustrations, and without my proofreader, Judy Bunch, this whole manuscript might have been incoherent.

I also must add that without the inspiration of my wife, Kay this would never have gotten off the ground, and I have a special salute to my son Sean, who not only gathered stories for me, but also lived them.

And last, but not least, thanks to the rest of my children, Patrick, Michelle, Christopher, Nicole and Tim, and the Boy Scouts of Troop 888 in Baton Rouge, who have been forced to listen to my ghost stories for years.